Exploring the Wilds of West Virginia:

A Hikers Guide to Beauty off the Beaten Path

Ed Rehbein

First published by Dog Ear Publishing
4011 Vincennes Rd
Indianapolis, IN 46268
www.dogearpublishing.net

ISBN: 978-1-4575-5101-7

This book is printed on acid-free paper.

Printed in the United States of America

Table of Contents

Part Five: Rivers Wild and Wonderful

Acknowledgments

Since this book is a compilation of some of the magazine articles that I have written for *Wonderful West Virginia* and *West Virginia South,* I owe much to the editors of these fine publications. When I started writing magazine articles, Lucia Hyde Robinson, editor of *Wonderful West Virginia,* gave me my first writing and photography assignment. It was an honor to be asked to contribute to such an outstanding magazine, and I am still humbled each time my work appears in it. Thank you, Lucia, for giving me my start. Sheila McEntee succeeded Lucia as managing editor of *Wonderful West Virginia,* and I am grateful for her support, encouragement, and impeccable editorial skills.

West Virginia South, a regional magazine that began circulation in October 2005, has also published some of the articles that appear in this book. I am grateful to the magazine's first managing editor, Lisa McMillion, for giving me a chance to write for the magazine. She also published my first cover photo, for which I will always be grateful. Her successor, Audrey Stanton, had a keen appreciation for the natural beauty of West Virginia, and I'm thankful that she kept me writing for *West Virginia South.*

Finally, I dedicate this book to Phyllis, my beloved wife, my constant companion, my best friend, and my fearless hiking partner, who has not once declined to venture with me off the beaten path and into uncharted territory. Together we've shared the thrill of discovering the wonderful sights of West Virginia described in this book.

I hope you enjoy them as much as we did!

Introduction

For hikers who like adventure and the thrill of discovery, this book is for you. Based on twenty years of exploring West Virginia's State Parks, National Parks, and Forest Service Lands, it's a guide to hidden waterfalls, little-known river trails, and unique vistas in West Virginia. Originally published as magazine articles, the 21 chapters in this guidebook carefully explain how to find trailheads and navigate your way off trail, too. What's more, GPS coordinates of key locations and trailheads are provided in the text and in a table at the end of the book. Everything is prepared for you to have a great time "Exploring the Wilds of West Virginia."

About the Author

Ed Rehbein is an award-winning writer and photographer focused on sharing with others the beauty of nature in Appalachia. He has published one book and more than 60 magazine articles exploring the natural beauties of West Virginia. He coauthored a book of photography called *West Virginia Waterfalls: The New River Gorge,* which was recognized as a "Finalist" in the "Photography Nature" category by the International Books Awards, 2011. Three of his magazine articles appearing in *Wonderful West Virginia* have won national awards by the Association for Conservation Information.

Part One

The West Virginia State Parks as Few People See Them

"Thousands of tired, nerve-shaken, over-civilized people are beginning to find out that going to the mountains is going home; that wildness is a necessity; and that mountain parks and reservations are useful not only as fountains of timber and irrigating rivers, but as fountains of life."

John Muir in Wild Wool (1875)

CHAPTER 1

Behind the Scenes at Babcock

Mention Babcock State Park in Fayette County and most people immediately think of the grist mill. And why not? The Glade Creek Grist Mill is one of the most photographed sights in West Virginia. You'll find pictures of the mill at Babcock on calendars and postcards—in magazines and travel brochures. The grist mill is a great ambassador of travel and tourism for southern West Virginia. Indeed more than 200,000 people visit Babcock every year.

Three Mills in One

The grist mill at Babcock is really three mills in one, which were salvaged from around the State–the Stoney Creek Grist Mill near Campbelltown in Pocahontas County, the Spring Run Grist Mill near Petersburg, and the Onego Grist Mill near Seneca Rocks in Pendleton County. Parts of each mill were disassembled piece-by-piece and reassembled on Glade Creek in Babcock. The reconstruction was completed in 1976. As mentioned in the Babcock State Park Brochure, the mill is a "living monument to the over 500 mills which thrived in West Virginia at the turn of the century."

But there's more to Babcock than the mill. You can rent paddle boats, canoes, or row boats on Boley Lake. The fishing is good at the lake or along Glade Creek. You can go hiking or horseback riding. And if you want to stay overnight, there's a 52-unit campsite, 13 standard log cabins, five standard cabins of frame construction, eight bungalow cabins, and two deluxe handicap accessible cabins. My family and I have stayed at the log cabins, and they are great. They're rustic, yet very comfortable. There are picnic grounds, a swimming pool, tennis courts and volleyball courts. All in all Babcock is a haven for outdoor recreation of all kinds.

Beauty Behind the Scenes

But there's still more to Babcock–behind the scenes so to speak. For years my wife Phyllis and I were content to hit the high spots at Babcock. It wasn't until a couple of years ago that we discovered a whole new dimension to Babcock. As it turns out, Babcock has some of the most interesting and diverse hiking trails in southern West Virginia. I'm not talking about off trail hiking, which we like to do. But rather there are some lesser known trails at Babcock that are loaded with scenic variety and interest. I'd like to tell you about one of them in this chapter–the Skyline Loop Trail.

The Skyline Loop Trail is really four trails in one–the Skyline, Rocky, Narrow Gauge, and Fisherman's Trails. Used together they form a great loop trail that has it all. On this loop you'll be treated to rock outcrops, several vistas of the Glade Creek Gorge, deep woods, small babbling brooks, the rocky cascades of Glade Creek, two swinging bridges, and depending upon the time of year, all the flowers that you can feast your eyes upon. All in three miles of trail!

The Skyline Trail

You can start the loop at any point. But I prefer to start at a trailhead for the Skyline Trail opposite Cabin #5 (GPS: Lat. 37.98336, Long. -80.94322). There's ample parking there, and this puts the hardest uphill stretch at the beginning of the hike. To me this is much better than lugging up a steep hill near the end of a long day of hiking. From the trailhead, hike about 500 feet until you reach the crest of the cliffs bordering the Glade Creek Canyon. Be on the lookout for an interesting wooden bridge on the trail that spans a deep crevasse in the sandstone cliffs. For the next half a mile or so the trail follows the cliff. As you walk the trail, watch for small side trails to the left. Many of these lead to sandstone slabs that jut out into the gorge. They provide lovely overlooks and panoramas of upper Glade Creek. My wife and I found five such overlooks–some better than others, but all worth a few extra steps of exploring through the brush.

If you're hiking in late May, look for Rhododendron and Azaleas. I know that Grandview Park is famous for its Rhododendron, but the trails of Babcock are every bit as good. The Manns Creek Gorge Trail always has lots of Rhody and Azalea. On the Skyline Trail in early June a couple of years ago, we found Mountain Laurel in blossom. They alone were worth the trip!

Do heed the warnings, though, of the Babcock Map and Trail Guide, which reads, "High cliff area–Watch your children carefully." Good advice.

After a short uphill stretch, the trail runs past a roadside overlook and a bench–a good place to take a breather and enjoy the view. From the overlook, your eyes can follow the course of Glade Creek and Manns Creek all the way down to the New River. But don't get too comfortable, there's more scenery ahead. From here to its junction with the Rocky Trail, the Skyline Trail has at least three more rocky overlooks. Again, just look for small side trails heading off to the left. My favorite overlook is the middle one, which is about a third of a mile beyond the roadside bench. It's on a flat, roomy sandstone ledge shaded by a pine tree and offers sweeping views of the upper and lower reaches of the Glade Creek Canyon.

The Rocky Trail

When reaching the intersection with the Rocky Trail, take it to the left. This is a wonderful little connector trail to get you from the cliff tops to the creek bottom. Rocky Trail is well named. You'll find hundreds of stone steps constructed by the Civilian Conservation Corps who built Babcock State Park in the mid 1930's. The trail follows a babbling brook as it descends into the gorge. The vertical drop is about 400 feet, which is why I prefer to go down the Rocky Trail rather than climb up it!

Near the creek bottom, the Rocky Trail intersects the Narrow Gauge Trail. Bear left and take the Narrow Gauge Trail about 1000 feet to a swinging bridge across Glade Creek. If you've packed a lunch, and I hope you have, this is a great lunch stop. Phyllis and I have munched a sandwich or two while dangling our legs over the edge of the bridge. It's not dangerous although we almost lost a plastic food container to the creek when it rolled off the bridge. Fortunately it got hung up on some rocks, and I retrieved it. It contained cookies, and I wasn't about to let them float away!

The Fisherman's Trail

After soaking up the scenery at the bridge, it's time for the last leg of the loop trail. It's the Fisherman's Trail, which follows Glade Creek back to the cabins. This is a mysterious trail in some respects. Sometimes it's listed on Babcock Trail Maps, and sometimes it isn't. It's shown on the paper copy of a trail map dated 2001, but it's not marked on the map that is downloadable from the Babcock State Park website. There's a good reason for this, and it's marked on a sign at the head of the trail: "TRAIL NOT MAINTAINED: Travel at your own risk." Likewise one brochure describes the trail this way: "Very rugged, difficult trail." Quite frankly, that doesn't discourage me; it merely piques my curiosity.

To be sure, the Fisherman's Trail is somewhat demanding, but it's great fun nevertheless. For one, it's a challenge to follow its trace as it winds along the creek. Sometimes, the trail wraps uphill around a huge boulder. At other times it slithers through Rhododendron thickets. In a few stretches it rides a path beneath steep overhanging sandstone cliffs. You'll even find a few stone steps–evidence again of the CCC. It's an old path, so trail blazes are few and faint. But it can be followed, and there's no chance of getting lost. Glade Creek is on your right the whole way, so if you merely "follow the river," so to speak, you'll find your way. Which is another reason for taking this trail; it follows the rocky course of Glade Creek, and allows you to see a part of Babcock that few of those 200,000 yearly visitors ever glimpse. The course of Glade Creek is strewn with rocky boulders, roaring cascades, small waterfalls, and pools of clear water. It's a delight to ear and eye.

The Fisherman's Trail runs for about a mile and a quarter from the swinging bridge at the Narrow Gauge Trail to another swinging bridge over Glade Creek opposite Cabin #5. Because of the rocky tread, it will seem like a longer distance, but it will be worth every step. From the second swinging bridge, take the stone steps up to Cabin #5. You'll find your vehicle at the trailhead parking behind the cabin.

All in all this loop trail is about three miles long, and it has it all–from high cliffs to a creek side scramble and everything in between. Best yet, it's untrammeled, unspoiled, and just waiting for you behind the scenes at Babcock.

Happy Trails!

CHAPTER 2

Jumping Off from Hawks Nest State Park: Exploring the sights outside the Park

Just below the lodge at Hawks Nest State Park, fabled Lovers Leap Rock juts out into the New River Gorge. It was there that, according to G.W. Swain, Little Swan, a Cherokee maiden, and Running Deer, a Shawnee brave, plunged to their deaths. As legend has it, because their parents opposed their marriage, the couple chose death together rather than life apart. These two young people transformed Lovers Leap into a dramatic "jumping off point." But there's another, safer, definition of a "jumping off point." It can also mean "a beginning from which an enterprise is launched, a point of departure, a springboard." In this sense, Hawks Nest State Park is indeed a splendid jumping off point, a base camp if you will, to explore several scenic gems in the hills and valleys outside the park.

To be sure, there's a lot to do at Hawks Nest. They have a lodge and dining room, a swimming pool, an aerial tram, a gift shop, a nature center, and a museum of Indian and pioneer artifacts. You can hike, fish, boat, and play tennis and basketball. You can even take a jet boat ride up Hawks Nest Lake to the New River Gorge Bridge. Even with these attractions, there's a lot more to enjoy nearby. In this chapter I'm going to highlight three especially interesting places that are easily reached from Hawks Nest State Park.

A Walk Through the Past

The first actually begins within the park boundaries. Called the Hawks Nest Trail, the southern end starts at the Nature Center at the base of the aerial tram and ascends along the banks of Mill Creek about 1.8 miles to the trail's end. The northern trailhead (GPS: Lat. 38.13070, Long. -81.10131) is located near the town of Ansted. Although beginning in the park, the trail is a project of the town of Ansted. According to Mayor Pete Hobbs, local contractors and town employees worked to refurbish the trail. The trail was opened to the public in the fall of 2004. It is part of a larger vision of the town of Ansted to develop its historical assets and coal heritage.

The trail follows the route of a narrow-gauge railroad built up the ravine of Mill Creek in 1874 by coal mine owners to connect their mines with the main line railroad on the New River. "A saddleback locomotive was used. In 1899, the Chesapeake and Ohio Railway (C&O) purchased the narrow gauge railroad and contracted with Colonel Page to do the work to upgrade the line to standard gauge, which was completed on August 20, 1890. C&O operated the new branch line, which was known as the Hawks Nest Subdivision . . . freight rail service on the branch line ended in 1972 and the tracks were removed" (Wikipedia Online Encyclopedia).

My wife Phyllis and I hiked this trail for the first time in June of 2005 and were impressed. A trailhead sign reads: "The property for this trail was given by Imperial Colliery Company in memory and in honor of all the miners who have worked in the coal seam situated along and lying between the New and Gauley Rivers of West Virginia." The trail does indeed honor and bring into remembrance the coal mining heritage of Ansted and environs. Hiking this trail you'll find old mine openings, two beautiful train trestles, and other remnants of the coal mining and rail service. This trail is well-marked by mileage posts and signs identifying points of interest.

Aside from historical interests, the trail boasts two waterfalls. One lies on Fox Branch, a small intermittent side stream about a half a mile up the trail from the bottom. The other straddles Mill Creek at about the one mile mark. The city of Ansted has scattered picnic tables and benches all along the trail. Indeed, the town of Ansted is to be commended for the vision and work they've put into this trail. Besides a wonderful walk in the woods, it's also an interesting stroll back to a time of bustling coal mines and railroads.

Cathedral Falls

The next point of interest I'd like to highlight is Cathedral Falls (GPS: Lat. 38.15389, Long. -81.17967). It's just six miles west from Hawks Nest State Park on U.S. Route 60 and is one of the most breathtaking falls in West Virginia. In *Waterfalls of Virginia and West Virginia,* Kevin Adams describes Cathedral Falls this way: "This is what people think about when they think about waterfalls. When the water is up, this one is about as good as it gets in West Virginia." I'd have to agree. The waters of Crane Branch, a tributary to the New River, tumble over 60 feet in a series of falls and dazzling cascades. Indeed, Cathedral Falls isn't one waterfall, it's many–each lovely in its own right.

One look at the falls and you'll know how it got its name. Steep-sided cliffs of stone enclose the falls like the walls of an ancient gothic cathedral. According to locals it's not unusual for couples to be wed at this outdoor temple of stone with its flowing fountain.

Another attractive feature of Cathedral Falls is its accessibility. Some of the more beautiful falls that I've seen in West Virginia are remote and take the resolve of a mountain goat to reach. But not the Cathedral. It's right off U.S. 60 at a little roadside rest about a mile east of Gauley Bridge. There's a covered picnic table, and the trail for viewing is wheel chair accessible. For that matter the falls can be seen quite nicely from the parking lot. This sight should be on everyone's map. It's lovely; it's approachable. It's well worth a visit.

The Hawks Nest Dam Trail

The third point of interest, the trail to Hawks Nest Dam, is also just six miles from Hawks Nest State Park. From the parking lot at

Hawks Nest take U.S. 60 west for three miles to the junction of WV Route 16 at Chimney Corner. Turn left onto Route 16 and go another three miles to the bridge crossing the New River at Cotton Hill. Just before crossing the bridge, turn into the trailhead parking area on the left (GPS: Lat. 38.11466, Long. - 81.14245).

The trail is owned and maintained by Brookfield Renewable Power. Before you venture on the trail, for safety sake remain alert and heed the warning signs posted by Brookfield which read:

> Warning! Dam Upstream. Water may rise rapidly at any time without warning. Siren will warn of definite water rise. Avoid placing yourself where quick exit from the river is difficult. Personal awareness at all times is required. Due to the noise from trains, water, and other environmental factors sirens may not always be heard. You are at risk to remain near the water after the water starts to rise or you hear a siren!

Forewarned is forearmed. Use common sense and always keep a healthy respect for potential hazards and dangers. This applies to all outdoor activities. Enjoy nature, but do it safely!

The New River Drys

That being said, the attractions of this trail are just too many and too fascinating to be passed over. Indeed, for a trail of only one mile, it's packed with interest. For instance, consider the New River, which has hewn a canyon some 600 to 900 feet deep through the backbone of the Appalachian Mountains in West Virginia. Then imagine what the cutting edge of the New River, that is, the mighty river bed would look like if laid bare. That's part of the attraction of the Hawks Nest Dam trail. For that's what you see. The awesome flow of the New River is held in check by the Hawks Nest Dam, but more than that, it's also diverted. The Hawks Nest Dam and reservoir, completed in 1934, force the waters of the New River to be channeled through a 40-foot-high tunnel for three miles underground through the mountain to a hydroelectric plant downstream. Most of the time the New River below the dam is merely a trickle, a shadow of its former self. This section of the New River Canyon is called the "New River Drys" for obvious reasons. And investigating this dry river bed is like walking in a geologic laboratory or a museum of natural history where the intricate forms and patterns of river scouring and erosion, which generally lie hidden beneath the surface of the river, are laid open and bare.

The river bed is accessed by three steep side trails for fishing at distances of 0.1, 0.5, and 0.6 miles from the trailhead. I don't know much about the fishing, but you can sure catch a lot of scenery. The river bed is a rocky platform of scoured sandstone well worth exploring. According to a publication written by Pete Lessing of the West Virginia Geologic and Economic Survey, the rock exposed in the river bed is called the Pineville Sandstone and is about 300 million years old. Prominent vertical joints or fractures crisscross the river bed carving the bedrock into blocks and boulders. And in some places, the river bed is so flat it resembles pavement.

What's more you can see evidence of the forces which laid down the sediments of the Pineville Sandstone. Ripple marks and cross-bedded sandstones record the action of the ancient rivers that laid down these sands.

If you're just interested in the sights at the base of Hawks Nest Dam, then skip the side trails and walk about 0.7 miles from the trailhead to the turnoff to the dam. A nicely graded trail takes you another 0.3 miles to the riverbed immediately below the dam where there awaits another fascinating geologic feature–giant monoliths. The bedrock below the dam is strewn with huge sandstone boulders, some thirty or more feet in height. To me they are sculptures in stone, carved with care by the New River, and then left for us to view after the waters of the river were diverted. There are paintings, too. The bedrock is often a canvas colored by nature with hues of red, gray, and brown. There's so much to explore along this trail that I doubt that one trip will satisfy your curiosity. Every time my wife and I revisit this trail, we leave full of enthusiasm for the sights it offers and with plans to return again.

For the lovelorn Indian couple, the legend of Lovers Leap didn't have a happy ending. But for hikers, nature lovers, and history buffs, Hawks Nest State Park can be a great jumping off point.

Happy landings!

CHAPTER 3

Extreme Pipestem: Chasing Waterfalls at Pipestem State Park

The highest waterfall in West Virginia might not be Blackwater Falls in Tucker County. And the best series of waterfalls might not be the Falls of Hills Creek in Pocahontas County. Both of these honors might very well belong to the Falls of Indian Branch in Pipestem Resort State Park of Monroe County. But you won't be able to see these falls or judge for yourself unless you're ready to do some extreme hiking!

Extreme Hikes

What is an extreme hike? It's a relatively new category of an expanding theme in outdoor sports–the challenge of the "Extreme." The ever-growing list of extreme sports includes base jumping, bungee jumping, hang gliding, kitesurfing, mountain biking, paragliding, rock climbing, roller skating, skateboarding, skydiving, snowboarding, whitewater canoeing, kayaking or rafting, and windsurfing. Extreme sports have their own TV channel, magazines, books, and websites.

Although extreme sports have been around for 10 years or so, interest in extreme hiking is just taking off. But back to our original question: What is an extreme hike? To some enthusiasts, it's a demanding day hike of long distance and dizzying ascents. But I don't believe extreme hikes should be limited to superbly conditioned youth. The young at heart can enjoy them, too.

To me extreme hikes can simply be hikes off existing trails. They're cross-country treks that take you over rocks, through natural tunnels, down climbing ladders, and across creeks. Some call it "bush-whacking," but it's not hacking your way through uncharted territory. It's merely following the traces forged by other outdoor enthusiasts such as rock climbers, kayakers, and yes, other extreme hikers!

Why go on an extreme hike? To enjoy scenic gems that are off the well-worn path. To be sure there's breathtaking scenery on marked trails. But there's so much more to be seen off the trail, and West Virginia is prime country for discovering beauties off the beaten path. Furthermore, you don't have to venture into Wilderness Areas or back pack for days to reach these hidden scenic gems. They're close at hand. Good examples are the waterfalls of Indian Branch in Pipestem State Park.

Pipestem State Park

Pipestem is one of the premier resorts in the West Virginia state park system. Accommodations include two lodges, McKeever Lodge on the cliff top and Mountain Creek Lodge by the banks of the Bluestone River, 26 fully equipped all weather deluxe cabins, and an 82-site campground. Amenities consist of two restaurants, a snack-bar, a sports lounge, an aerial tram, three gift shops, and a conference center. In addition, Pipestem features two golf courses–an 18-hole par 72 championship course and a challenging 9-hole par 3 course. There's also horseback riding, swimming, archery, fishing, paddle boating, canoeing, bicycling, lighted basketball courts, horseshoes, hiking, picnicking, and, at nearby Bluestone Wildlife Management area, hunting. With all this, it's easy to see why Pipestem is called the "Year round Crown Jewel of West Virginia State Parks."

Diamonds in the Rough

But among the "jewels" of Pipestem lie some diamonds in the rough, which you'll never see unless you venture off the trail for an extreme hike. The "diamonds" I'm referring to are the waterfalls along Indian Branch. Here's how to find them. Take the County Line Trail, which begins at the Nature Center (GPS: Lat. 37.52466, Long. -80.98839). A sign below the trail marker warns: "CAUTION: The hike to and from Indian Branch Falls via the County Line Trail will require a long steep and strenuous ascent near the end of the walk." Sounds like an extreme hike already, but that sign is just referring to the part of the hike that's on the trail!

A steep 1.2 miles descent along the County Line Trail leads to the top of Indian Branch Falls. Unfortunately, the only view is a narrow glimpse from a small, fenced observation point above the falls. It's an enticing peek, however, of an impressive fall. There's about a 30-foot plunge down an overhanging cliff, a short rocky run, and then another horsetail falls of about 15 feet in height. The falls sit center-stage in a U-shaped amphitheater formed by rugged, sandstone cliffs. It'd be quite a sight if you could get to the base of the falls, but the massive overhanging cliffs are daunting. They seem to guard this glistening jewel. Like a diamond under glass, you can admire the falls, but only from afar. Fortunately with some off-trail bushwhacking and extreme hiking you can enjoy these falls up close.

From the signpost for the observation point of the falls continue 180 paces or about 450 feet down the County Line Trail until you come to a small gully. Look for a faint foot path curling off to the left and down the gully. Leaving the main trail, take this path, and prepare yourself for a little adventure, a bit of extreme hiking, and some breathtaking scenery.

Upper Indian Branch Falls

The foot path descends steeply down a V-shaped gully. In hiking off the trails in West Virginia, my wife and I have noticed that small side streams often cut notches in seemingly impassable sandstone cliffs that can be negotiated by hikers willing to expend the effort. Fortunately, this little stream has cut a notch in the sandstone cliffs, and after a rocky decline of some 60 feet, you'll come to the base of the cliff.

At this point the waterfall seems accessible since the main hurdle has been overcome, but making the correct approach to the falls is crucial. Plunging headlong down the slope until you reach the stream leads straight into thick underbrush and dense Rhododendron. And if you have the fortitude to make this traverse, you'll be faced with slippery going on the rocks of the stream bed. In exploring the cliffs of the New River Gorge, my wife and I have discovered that easier routes run along the base of sandstone cliffs.

This is the case here. From the gully, bear left (upstream) and hug the cliffs along their base. The way is level and leads right to the base of the falls. The falls are accessible from all sides and offer prime opportunities for photography. On the left, as you're facing the falls, you can get close profile views of the falls. From the right, the profile views open up revealing more of the sandstone amphitheater. And in the center you can photograph both the main plunge and horsetail falls together. Right, left, or center, the falls are a beautiful sight. You'll be glad you hiked through the rough to see this diamond!

Lower Indian Branch Falls

But there's more to Indian Branch. Indeed the Lower Falls of Indian Branch are higher and prettier, and yes, harder to get to. But nothing an extreme hiker can't handle. After you've soaked in the beauty of the upper falls, backtrack along the cliff base to the gully that you descended. If you've had enough for one day, hike back up the gully to the County Line Trail and return by the way you came. But if you're ready to chase another waterfall, lace up your boots and get ready for a steep descent.

In *Waterfalls of Virginia and West Virginia,* author Kevin Adams, a waterfall hunter of renown, wrote: "Below Indian Branch Falls, the creek spills over many other waterfalls before dumping into the Bluestone. The park naturalist estimates the next one down at 65 feet high. Unfortunately, there is no trail and the bushwhacking is extremely tough." That is nothing less than an invitation for waterfall chasing, extreme hiking, and high adventure!

Head downhill keeping to the top of the right-hand bank of the gully. You'll probably see the faint path of extreme hikers who've forged the way. Continuing down slope, you'll reach Indian Branch. At this point the stream bed is flat, sandstone bedrock with few boulders. Tread easy on this surface because it forms the lip of the Lower Falls of Indian Branch. You can view the falls from this lip, but please be careful. The rocks are very slippery. Just like the Upper Falls, the Lower Falls are formed by a massive, overhanging sandstone, but in a larger and higher U-shaped amphitheater. Getting to the base of the Lower Falls looks even more intimidating than getting to the Upper Falls.

But another side-stream has carved a way to the bottom. Just climb out of the stream bed and hike above the cliff on the northern slope of the stream valley. Contouring along the slope for about 350 feet, you'll come to another small gully, which breaks the cliff. It's a steep but manageable descent. Pass up the cliff base on this route; it's a little too risky. Instead continue down the gully to the creek bed. Watch the rocks as you walk up the creek to the falls. They don't see much sunlight and are very slippery. Buy a good walking stick to steady you, or better yet, join the Department of Natural Resources "Hiking West Virginia" program. After logging 25 miles on State Park and Forest trails, you'll receive a free wooden hiking stick.

The Lower Falls have everything a waterfall chaser could ask for–a grand amphitheater, a segmented fall with two steep plunges (one more than 40 feet high), mesmerizing, stair-step cascades in the lower reaches, and a small but picturesque plunge pool. These falls are more than 60 feet high overall and rank as one of the tallest in West Virginia. It's a rare feast for the eyes and the camera. I've never seen published pictures of this waterfall, so savor the sight and do take some photos back with you. The backtrack to the Nature Center requires a steep climb of 300 vertical feet back to the County Line Trail and another 400 vertical feet to reach the trailhead. It's a strenuous haul back to the parking lot, but the thrill of the adventure will put a bounce in your step.

A Taste of Adventure

In our technology-driven world, I think many hunger for a taste of adventure in the great outdoors. For many people, extreme sports fills this void. But so can extreme hiking. If you're willing to venture off the beaten path, there's much to gain. You'll discover beauty and wonder in familiar places. You'll develop a greater sense of self-reliance, of being able to literally think on your feet. You'll learn to gauge your abilities and judge risks. And you'll have the indescribable pleasure of discovering a scenic jewel–a diamond in the rough.

So take an extreme hike in West Virginia. You'll find that it's a scenic treasure chest.

CHAPTER 4

The Road Less Traveled: Three State Parks Off the Beaten Path

Pipestem, Blackwater, Canaan, Stonewall, these names are well-known in the West Virginia State Park system. They're visited by thousands each year. But what of the lesser known parks? In this chapter, we'll highlight three of the more out-of-way state parks and forests. As it turns out, they have a lot to offer for those who dare to venture off the beaten path.

Kumbrabow State Forest

Nestled high in the mountains of southern Randolph County, Kumbrabow State Forest is definitely off the beaten path. Its 9,500 acres straddle Rich Mountain and range in elevation from 3,000 to 3,900 feet, making Kumbrabow the highest state forest. From the south it's about five miles to Kumbrabow on a gravel road out of Monterville, WV, and from the east it's four miles from U.S. 219 out of the town of Elkwater (GPS: Lat. 38.63292, Long. -80.02257).

You have to work to get to Kumbrabow, but it's worth it. Indeed, seclusion is part of its charm. Kumbrabow offers something you can't find in the high-tech world of cable TV, cell phones, and palm pilots—a chance to slow down and experience at an unhurried pace the unspoiled beauty of forests and streams.

For example, there are five rustic log cabins at Kumbrabow. They're grouped in a grassy meadow adjacent to Mill Creek, which forms a lovely waterfall at the north end of the cabin area complete with swimming hole and rope swing. All the cabins have fireplaces, wood-burning kitchen stoves, gas lanterns and refrigerators and come equipped for housekeeping. But what they do not have makes them as interesting as what they do have. They don't have running water or electricity. That's right. No TV's blaring; no boom boxes booming–just the gentle trickle of the creek and the murmur of leaves rustling in the wind. The solitude is so pure you'll find yourself whispering.

By the way, each cabin is close to a pump for water and has its own clean pit toilet. My family and I have stayed at similar rustic cabins at another West Virginia state forest, and I must say that what seems lacking in amenities is more than made up for by the charm of drawing your own water from a well and reading or playing cards by lantern light in the evening.

Kumbrabow also has 13 rustic campsites hugging Mill Creek. And for all registered campers and cabin guests, there's a shower and a laundry at the park headquarters. There's also a wheel chair accessible camp site and cabin.

When you're not enjoying the solitude, there's plenty to see and do at Kumbrabow. There's picnicking, hiking, hunting, and fishing. About 400 acres of the forest lands have been set aside for recreation. Indeed, Kumbrabow offers unique trout fly-fishing packages, which include cabin rental and lessons on the nearby Elk River by a reputable, licensed, trout fishing guide. Within the park, there's good fishing for native brook trout along Mill Creek.

Although hunting is forbidden within the developed areas of Kumbrabow, thousands of acres of state forest remain open to hunters, and they should be pleased with their prospects. Because of its remoteness and healthy timber lands, Kumbrabow State Forest is a wildlife haven. According to the state forest brochure, "deer, bear, turkey, bobcat and ruffed grouse are the most prevalent game in the forest."

If you're not packing a rod or a rifle, you can always hike on the 12 miles or so of trails. Some of the trails lead along streams. Many take you to ridge tops for spectacular vistas. On all of them you'll see West Virginia forests at their finest–lush and green and rich in variety. Located in the heart of the mountains of West Virginia, Kumbrabow also makes a good base from which to explore other areas such as, Snowshoe, Cass, and Cheat Mountain.

Rustic often implies rough and unkempt, but this isn't the case at Kumbrabow. It's clean, well-maintained, and immaculately groomed. If you're looking for a break from this fast-paced world, a trip to Kumbrabow could be just what you need.

Camp Creek State Forest and Park

Hunting, fishing, camping, hiking, horseback riding–what's not to like about Camp Creek? Located in Mercer County in the southern part of the State, Camp Creek is a haven for the outdoor enthusiast. Although it doesn't receive as many visitors as nearby Pipestem or Bluestone State Parks, it's not because it's isolated. The Camp Creek entrance (GPS: Lat. 37.50368, Long. -81.12774) is only two miles off exit 20 of Interstate 77. So Camp Creek is easy to find, but it's not easy to leave because there's just so much to do.

Actually Camp Creek is more than a state park; it's a state forest, too. In 1987, 550 acres of state forest lands were set aside for the development of recreation. Thus began Camp Creek State Park. Adjacent to the park, the remaining 5300 acres of state forest support and supplement the recreational activities of the park.

Indeed one of the more exciting features of Camp Creek State Park capitalizes on the forest lands. I'm referring to 14 equestrian camp sites, which accommodate both horses and humans. Opening on July 9, 2004, there's space for horse trailers and campers. The equestrian site is located on the northern border of the state park and is a perfect access point for more than 25 miles of trails and roads that crisscross the state forest. You won't get lost in the forest either because new maps generated by GPS surveys are now available. By the way, the equestrian sites at Camp Creek are the first of their kind in the West Virginia State Park system. But be sure to plan ahead. Sites are by reservation only.

If you'd rather explore nature on two feet rather than four, there's a fine system of hiking trails and lots to see. One of my favorite parts of the park are the waterfalls–Mash Fork and Campbell Falls. Campbell Falls is an easy 0.3 mile hike along a gravel road bordering Camp Creek. This cataract stair-steps over rock ledges and falls about 15 feet in overall height. It's as pretty as a picture so take your camera. And if you'd like to beat the heat of a hot summer day, slip on some old tennis shoes and walk the creek bed above the falls. The water isn't deep, and it runs over flat bedrock sandstone. With a canopy of green leaves overhead and cool water underfoot, you'll forget all about the heat of summer.

If you prefer waders to wading, there's plenty of opportunities for fishing at Camp Creek. According to the Superintendent, "Camp Creek is one of the best stocked trout streams in the state." Hunting is popular in the state forest, and mountain bikers are welcome to use the trails and roads.

I guess it's not surprising that camping is a large part of Camp Creek. There are two camp sites. At the Mash Fork campground there are 26 trailer/tent sites with electrical hookup, heated bathhouse, and two wheelchair accessible sites. The Blue Jay campground is more rustic with 12 sites for tents. With five large picnic shelters, Camp Creek is great for family reunions and large gatherings. Tables are scattered throughout the park for small groups, too. Twice a year, in the spring and fall, the park hosts festivals, which are free to the public.

All in all there's a lot to see and do at Camp Creek. It's well worth the trip.

Beartown State Park

Our Nation's Capital may be known for its museums and fine art galleries, but nestled in the hills of Pocahontas County, there lies a Museum of both Natural History and Art that rival any Washington has to offer. I'm referring to Beartown State Park, a 107-acre natural preserve perched on the eastern slopes of Droop Mountain seven miles south of Hillsboro on U.S. 219 (Park Location GPS: Lat. 38.05152, Long. -80.27526). The park was established in 1970 with funds from the Nature Conservancy and a donation from Mrs. Edwin G. Polan in memory of her son, Ronald Keith Neal, who lost his life in the Vietnam War.

Rocks, picturesque and beautiful, are the main attractions at Beartown. Composed of the Droop Mountain Sandstone, these rocks have been carved by time and the elements into angular boulders, rounded stones, and narrow crevices. The crevices crisscross the area dividing the bedrock into large stone islands. The intersecting crevices resemble streets, and the stone islands look like city blocks. Couple this with a natural habitat for bears in the clefts and caves, and you have the name Beartown.

To preserve the natural beauty of Beartown and make it more accessible, boardwalks and wooden steps wind through the rock crevasses. There's even a board walk accessible by wheelchair. The boardwalks, which serve as your guide through this outdoor museum, begin at the top of the rocks and gradually descend downslope and into the rock clefts. Along the way, you'll also find well-written and informative plaques describing the natural processes at work in Beartown.

The boardwalk begins by weaving between massive blocks of sandstone. The display of stone is awesome and diverse. Some of the blocks are angular while others are softly rounded. Slabs of stone rest upon one another at uneasy angles. Vertical rock walls give way to gravity defying overhangs. Many of the rock monoliths are capped by lush green ferns.

As you descend the boardwalk, the crevices seem to narrow and the rock walls get taller. At some point it seems as if you're walking down the corridors of an elaborate art gallery, the walls of which have been decorated by nature. Red and brown stains due to the weathering of iron-bearing minerals paint the rock walls as well as any human artist could. Sculptures abound as well. Irregularities in the cementation of the sandstone have been accentuated by the elements. Water and ice have slowly but surely worn away the stone. The softer zones of the rock have been hollowed out leaving a dazzling array of vertical and horizontal flutes, narrow ridges, and rounded hollows, holes, and pits.

If this wasn't enough to captivate the eye, moss covers many of the rock walls coating the finely sculptured surfaces in Kelly green. One such narrow corridor is so lavishly draped in moss that is deserves the name, "The Emerald Aisle."

At Beartown, rocks and plants have combined their talents to create a diamond in the rough, a jewel of nature nestled in the hills of West Virginia. Your only regret at Beartown will be the end of the boardwalk signaling that your tour is over. The park is open daily from April to October and may be visited in the off season by contacting the Park Superintendent.

In a poem entitled "The Road Not Taken," Robert Frost wrote: "Two roads diverged in a wood, and I–I took the one less traveled by, And that has made all the difference." This could well apply to West Virginia state parks. The road less traveled might make all the difference to you.

CHAPTER 5

Watoga in Winter

A couple of inches of snow lay on the ground, and icicles hung from the roof. The temperatures lingered in the 20's, and the sun was shrouded by slate-gray clouds. It was a typical winter day in the middle of February, and my wife Phyllis and I couldn't have been more content. Why? We were sitting around a warm hearth being serenaded by wood crackling in a fireplace. In our hands were books that, up till now, we could never quite find the time to read. But with no appointments to make or phones to answer, we had time to do the things we'd put off. We were snug in a cabin at Watoga State Park. And as we learned, contentment in a cabin seems to come easily. We had discovered Watoga in winter.

A Mid-Winter Vacation

Last winter, Phyllis and I revived an old tradition of ours called the "Mid-Winter Vacation." We're primarily hikers, and since neither of us are into skiing, either downhill or cross-country, winter often puts a halt to our travel and enjoyment of the outdoors. In the past to break the monotony of winter, we'd take our two children Matt and Angela to a local state park, such as Pipestem or Twin Falls, and rent a cabin for the weekend. It was a pleasant getaway and a great opportunity to slow down and enjoy time together.

In February of this year our interest in a Mid-Winter vacation was rekindled while looking over winter specials at certain West Virginia

State Parks. The discount rates at Watoga State Park looked especially good–stay three nights and receive 50% off the total price. That was too good to pass up. We booked three nights and had a grand time.

Watoga–Lost in Translation But Easy to Find

In case you're not familiar with Watoga State Park, it's about a two-hour drive from Beckley, WV. The drive isn't difficult. You go east on I-64 to Lewisburg and take U.S. 219N for about 25 miles to Hillsboro. The west entrance to the park (GPS: Lat. 38.12679, Long. -80.17384) is just two miles off U.S. 219. The north entrance (GPS: Lat. 38.11388, Long. -80.09316) is eight miles south of the intersection of State Route 39 and Huntersville.

Perhaps another way to locate the park is to look at its name–Watoga. Everyone agrees that it's derived from the Cherokee word, "Watauga." But that's where the agreement ends. Nobody is quite sure what "Watauga" really means. The first source I examined stated that "Watauga" means "river of islands." This made good sense to me since the "river of islands," in this case, is the Greenbrier River whose many shallow stretches leave scattered islands in the river. And since the Greenbrier River borders the park on the west and is a major attraction, Watoga seems like an ideal name for the park. But an article entitled "What in the world is 'Watauga?'" published in the *Mountain Times* in Boone, North Carolina and online by Allan Scherlen, Librarian at Appalachian State University, muddied the waters so to speak about the true translation of "Watauga." After extensive research, Mr. Scherlen concluded that you can take your pick among these choices: "beautiful waters, beautiful water, running waters, falling water, whispering waters, clear waters, flowing water, river of plenty, foaming at the mouth, broken waters, village of many springs, river of islands . . ." With the exception of "foaming at the mouth," I find all these possible meanings charming and quite descriptive of the Greenbrier River as it flows by Watoga State Park and through Southern West Virginia. Indeed, the meaning of "Watauga" might have been lost in translation, but the State Park is easy to find and appreciate.

Year-Round Recreation

Covering 10,100 acres in Pocahontas County, Watoga is West Virginia's largest state park. Combined with the 9,400 acres of Calvin Price State Forest, which adjoins Watoga to the south, there's plenty of public land and many ways to enjoy year-round recreation. Watoga operates three separate campgrounds: Beaver Creek, Riverside, which lies along the Greenbrier River, and Laurel Run. Several years ago, my mom and step-dad drove their RV all the way from Oregon to visit us. We stayed at the Riverside Campground. My mom and step-dad and our kids slept in the RV while my wife and I pitched a tent. My best memory is playing in the shallow waters of the Greenbrier River with the kids. In total there are 88 camp sites. Beaver Creek and Riverside Campgrounds are open from spring to late fall. If camping is not your thing, Watoga has 34 cabins. Twenty-four standard cabins are constructed of log and stone and are rented from the last weekend in April to the end of October. I have some friends at Church that rent a cabin at Watoga in the fall to enjoy the autumn foliage. The ten modern cabins are frame construction. Two of these cabins are ADA accessible. They feature wood paneled walls, a gas furnace, and a stone fireplace. The modern cabins are open all year, which is fortunate, because Watoga can be a winter playground as well.

A Winter Playground

To be sure, many of the summer facilities such as the swimming pool, the game courts, and the restaurant are closed for the winter. But that doesn't prevent Watoga from being a winter playground. In winter many of the trails and some of the unplowed roads are converted into cross-country ski routes. Although not all of the 40 miles of hiking trails are suitable for cross-country skiing, there should be plenty of opportunities to enjoy the park on skis or snowshoes. And don't forget the Greenbrier River Trail on the west side of the park. Built on an old railroad bed following the river, the grade is very gentle and even. Phyllis and I enjoyed hiking along the river on the Greenbrier River Trail. The partially frozen waters of the

Greenbrier formed fascinating patterns. We also enjoyed watching a small flock of Canada geese swim in the river and preen themselves on the ice. Snow-draped trees and rocks decorated with icicles added to the artistry of nature in winter. A mile and a half hike around a frozen Watoga Lake showed off more of winter's wonders. Grass and reeds along the shore bowed their heads as if in slumber while waiting for the warmth of spring. While circling the lake, we saw several people ice fishing–yet another way to enjoy Watoga in winter. According to park personnel, bass are often found at the end of those fishing lines.

Surrounding Attractions

Watoga is also a convenient base from which to explore surrounding attractions. For example, many winter guests stay at the cabins in Watoga in order to ski the slopes at the Snowshoe Mountain Resort, which is about 35 miles north of the park. For a few extra miles of driving, these skiers save a lot on lodging. The Green Bank National Radio Astronomy Observatory is also about 35 miles north of Watoga. During the winter and spring the Observatory is open to the public Thursday through Monday from 10 am to 6 pm. Call 304-456-2150 or email gbt-tours@nrao.edu for more information. At the town of Hillsboro just two miles from the park's western entrance stands the childhood home of Pearl S. Buck, the first American woman to win both the Pulitzer and Nobel Prizes for literature. During January and February, guided tours of the Pearl S. Buck House are offered Sunday at 1 pm and 2 pm, Monday through Friday at 1pm, and Saturday at 11 am, 1 pm, and 2 pm. If you have questions, please contact Curator Marie Toner at 215-249-0100 x149 or email to mtoner@pearlsbuck.org. Droop Mountain Battlefield State Park and Beartown State Park are just five and seven miles, respectively, south of Hillsboro on U.S. 219. Droop Mountain is the site of an historic Civil War battle and Beartown hosts some highly unusual rock formations. Droop Mountain is open during the winter, and Beartown may be seen in the off season by contacting the Superintendent of Droop Mountain Battlefield State Park.

The Cabin Life

But if you're not interested in sight seeing, you can happily wile away the hours at Watoga. All the cabins have fireplaces, electric lighting, modern kitchen appliances and bathrooms with showers. And they come completely equipped for housekeeping. But what the cabins do NOT have makes them as interesting as what they do have. You won't hear any televisions blaring, or phones ringing. And if you leave your computer at home, all you'll have to listen to is the quiet crackling of wood burning in the fireplace. There's something to be said for simply hunkering down in a cozy cabin in the woods in the middle of winter and just relaxing. Last year Phyllis and I brought a few books, our set of dominoes, and some of our favorite snacks, and that was more than enough to fill our cabin at Watoga with contentment.

If a mid-winter vacation sounds good to you, why not try Watoga, and discover for yourself why the park brochures say, "There's no time like snow time at Watoga."

Part Two:

New Places in the New River Gorge

"I only went out for a walk, and finally concluded to stay out till sundown, for going out, I found, was really going in."

From John of the Mountains:
The Unpublished Journals of John Muir

CHAPTER 6

Hidden Treasures of the New River Gorge
Five Waterfalls off the Beaten Path

We heard the waterfall before we saw it and heaved a sigh of relief. Worn, ragged, a bit bruised, but not beaten, my wife Phyllis and I had just struggled for two and a half hours to cover a mere half a mile. We were accustomed to hiking off-trail along the base of the cliffs that rim the New River Gorge, but this stretch of cliff-line was more than we bargained for. Yet, we were closing in. We hugged the cliffs that towered above us as we scrambled around yet another set of moss-covered boulders. With each step the roar of water grew louder until we were face-to-face with our quarry–a stream of water taking a 70-foot leap off the top ledge of the New River Gorge. For pure drama it was hard to beat. What's more, this waterfall, rivaling the height of any waterfall in West Virginia and, to be sure, the tallest in the New River Gorge, was not on any trail map either in print or on the web. Yet there we were, photographing, sketching and munching lunch next to this awesome yet virtually unknown waterfall. This experience confirmed what Phyllis and I have learned over the last 26 years of living in Southern West Virginia, that when exploring the New River Gorge both adventure and discovery come standard with every foray off the beaten path. These out-of-the-way waterfalls of the New River Gorge are hidden treasures just waiting to be discovered and admired. Let me share five of my favorites with you.

Tracking down these waterfalls won't require a lot of road time. All five are concentrated within a mile radius of the National Park Service (NPS) Trailhead at Kaymoor Top (GPS: Lat. 38.04601, Long. -81.06837) near Fayetteville, WV. As a bonus, the falls are just a mile southeast of the world famous New River Gorge Bridge. Your best bet is to pick up "Trails of the New River" at the Canyon Rim Visitor Center on U.S. 19 at the north end of the bridge. I'll refer to this NPS map for directions.

Tips for Hiking Below the Cliffs

Let's start this waterfall safari with the one described above, which is at the head of Craig Branch. Being the tallest in the New River Gorge, I've dubbed it the "Queen of the Gorge." From the Kaymoor Top Trailhead take the Kaymoor Miners Trail (#9). After a few gentle switchbacks, you'll descend a set of wooden steps. Below the steps you'll pass a small waterfall on your right. As you turn to head directly downhill on some rock steps, you'll parallel a small stream. On this stretch of the trail look for a faintly worn but distinguishable path to the right that crosses the little creek and heads toward the nearby cliffs. As you venture on this course, you truly step off the beaten path of NPS groomed, marked, and maintained trails and commit yourself to the rugged realm of rock climbers. Forged by rock climbers who come to scale the awesome sandstone cliffs of the New River Gorge, there are many such unmarked paths running along the base of the cliffs. These trails lead to spectacular sights most of which are not plotted on traditional maps or guides to the gorge. Thankfully, you don't need to be a rock climber to hike them, but these cliff-hugging trails do demand that you watch your step and keep your wits.

Here are some tips to help you negotiate the trail to the "Queen" at the head of Craig Branch. Keep in mind that the trail is not a trail at all. It's merely a set of paths forged by others and cleared by usage. These paths constantly diverge and converge, so following them can be confusing. Following a path beside a cliff base that is level and straight is easy. But often a cliff line is interrupted by changes in level or by breaks in the cliff face, which are difficult to negotiate. Likewise, boulder fields and rhododendron thickets can confuse the way and hinder progress. After much trial and error, Phyllis and I have learned that when picking your way through these difficult stretches, the chief rule of thumb is: "Hug the cliffs." Even if staying close to the cliff means more ups and downs, resist the temptation to strike out on the level across boulder fields. Last Spring along this very traverse, I nearly broke my leg when I stepped into a hole half way up my calf while crossing a boulder field littered with leaves. I managed to extricate my leg just before falling flat on my chest. Despite some hazards, you need not fear getting lost. The cliffs are unmistakable landmarks pointing the way both forward and back.

To the Queen and Back

With these tips in mind, the way to the Queen can be found by following the base of the cliff. Along the way, you'll be rewarded by dazzling displays of the Endless Wall, a massive, vertical to overhanging cliff of sandstone more than 120 feet high that rims the gorge for many miles upstream and down. When you're close enough to the waterfall to hear it, be watchful for a portion of the trail that gradually steepens and appears to be taking you up and into a cleft near the top of the cliff. At the apex of the debris cone formed by soil and rock being channeled through the cleft, the most obvious trail continues up into the cleft. Don't take this path now, but don't forget it either. At its apex, follow the cone along the cliff down the opposite side. After a few more rocky traverses, you'll find yourself perched overlooking Upper Craig Branch Falls. Regardless of the difficulty of the journey, seeing the waterfall will lift your spirits.

Now about the way back; I admit that the traverse from the Kaymoor Miners Trail wore Phyllis and me down. We were dreading the return trip. But fortune favored the bold that day. The path up the cleft, which I mentioned before, turned out to be a short cut back to the trailhead. If you climb the steep trail up the cleft, you'll reach the top of the cliffs. From the top of the cliff, descend the small ridge in front of you. There's no trail at this point. Simply follow your feet downhill for six or seven hundred feet until you reach a gravel road, which is the NPS Craig Branch Trail (#10). Turn right on the road and in a little less than a mile you will be back at the Kaymoor Top Trailhead–tired but happy. You'll have found a scenic treasure of the New River Gorge that few others have beheld.

Upper Falls of Butcher Branch

Opposite the Craig Branch Trail at the far end of the Kaymoor Top parking lot lays another pathway to discovery–the NPS Butcher Branch Trail (#11). Though you don't have to bushwhack to it, I consider the lovely Upper Falls of Butcher Branch to be off the beaten path because it receives little or no mention in tourist guides, maps in print or on the web, or in NPS literature. Here's how to find it. From the Kaymoor Top Trailhead, take the Butcher Branch Trail (#11). The trail runs along the top of the cliffs for a bit before gradually descending into a notch in the cliffs cut by Butcher Branch. After a switchback or two, the trail forks. The Butcher Branch Trail continues on the left fork and in a quarter mile connects to the NPS Long Point Trail (#12). Take the right fork labeled "Climber Access." Unlike the way to Craig Branch, this is a trail! It leads to rock climbing areas beyond Butcher Branch. After several switchbacks that descend the cliff and a brief walk through the woods, the trail crosses Butcher Branch. Above the crossing, Butcher Branch rolls down a steep, irregular, rock face in a series of picturesque cascades and drops that are well worth a photograph or two. Linger as long as you please, for it's only a half a mile hike back to the parking lot.

The Middle Falls of Fern Creek

The next two waterfalls, the Upper and Middle Falls of Fern Creek, lie on the opposite side of the gorge. From the Kaymoor Trailhead, return to Fayetteville, cross the New River Gorge Bridge on U.S. 19, and stop at the NPS Canyon Rim Visitor Center. When the leaves are off and the water is high, such as in springtime, the Middle Falls of Fern Creek can be spotted by those traveling north across the New River Bridge. It's on the right-hand side about halfway down the canyon. The waterfall seems to just leap out of the gorge. It's quite a sight; one I'm sure thousands of travelers have viewed from afar. Yet, I'd wager that in a year's time only a couple dozen ever see the falls up close.

Here's how to become one of those few. From the Visitor Center, turn right out of the parking lot and drive two-tenths of a mile. Make a very sharp right hand turn, and proceed downhill a tenth of a mile to a junction with the Fayette Station Road. Turn left and go three-tenths of a mile to a pull out on the right-hand shoulder of the road. This is the trailhead parking (GPS: Lat. 38.06756, Long. -81.07188). One path takes off from the shoulder of the road and heads straight downhill. But for an easier descent, take an old road that starts a few yards to the left. This is also a climber's access trail, but it's much easier to follow than the one to Craig Branch. You'll cross a little stone bridge and pass a small, seasonal waterfall. The trail follows this creek downhill a short way and then cuts to the left and uphill slightly. Follow the path to the base of some sandstone cliffs, which are also a part of the Endless Wall. The trail is neither marked nor maintained, but it's kept clear primarily by usage. Just remember to hug the cliffs whenever possible. The scenery along the cliffs is striking. The sandstones of the cliff face have been etched and sculptured by the slow but sure hand of Nature and in many places are exquisitely stained in multiple tones of brown and red by the gentle brush strokes of weathering.

After hugging the cliffs for about 4/5 of a mile, you depart from the trail to do some serious bushwhacking to the Middle Falls of Fern Creek. If you're hiking in early spring when trees are bare, you should be able to spot the waterfall for the first time. It'll be downhill and to the left if you are facing downhill. At this point, I've scratched two arrows on a boulder on the ground pointing downhill. The hunt begins here. The slope drops about 400 vertical feet in a 500-foot horizontal run. That's a little less than a 45-degree angle, which is, needless to say, steep. So be forewarned. Fortunately there are no cliffs to scale or rhododendron thickets to negotiate. But the way is still tough. The slope is rocky and covered with grass and underbrush.

When you reach the falls, you'll know why they can be seen from the New River Bridge. At the top of the falls Fern Creek hits a stony, horizontal ramp that launches it into the air and sends it streaming down to the boulders below. It's rugged; it's raw; it's breathtaking. Fern Creek continues its rocky descent into the gorge with more spectacular cascades and falls, but let's leave those for another time. The Upper Falls of Fern Creek are waiting. The best way back up to the trail is to retrace your footsteps.

High Drama at Upper Fern Creek Falls

When you return to the trail at the foot of the cliffs, it's only another fifth of a mile to the Upper Falls of Fern Creek. Just turn right and continue on the trail at the base of the cliffs. The waterfall announces itself with a roar that echoes off the rock walls as you approach it. My jaw dropped the first time I saw this waterfall. It sits center-stage in a stone amphitheater enclosed on three sides. It's high drama for sure. Most of the time the falls are confined to a vertical cleft cut in the cliffs. But at high water, the falls make a spectacular plunge off the cliff top and into a pool in the middle of the amphitheater. It's clearly one of the best sights in the New River Gorge. The backtrack to the trailhead is about a mile. You might be a bit foot-weary, but if you've caught the thrill of discovery in the New River Gorge, you'll be pondering your next waterfall hunt.

Lying in Wait: Wolf Creek Falls

Wolf Creek is well named. It's wild, intimidating, and untamed. It charges down the slopes of the New River Gorge like a wild animal. Not surprisingly, Wolf Creek Falls are rough and rugged, too. Fortunately, you don't have to hike far to find them because they're just off a paved road. But as if lying in wait, they are quite hidden from the road, and undoubtedly thousands of visitors to the gorge drive right by them unaware of the awesome waterfall just a few feet from them.

To find this hidden treasure of the gorge, you'll need to drive into the New River Gorge and back out again. Starting from the trailhead to Fern Creek Falls, reverse direction and drive downhill. At about three-tenths of a mile, bear left at a junction. This puts you on Fayette Station Road, a one-way, paved road that switchbacks its way down the north side of the New River Gorge and up the south side. The road goes under the New River Gorge Bridge twice, crosses the New River on Fayette Station Bridge, and has numerous views of the gorge and the river. Four-wheel drive isn't needed for this road, and it's the best route by car to get a feel for the beauty and majesty of the New River Gorge. As you ascend the south side of the gorge look for a trailhead in the middle of a very wide switchback. This is the trailhead parking for NPS Fayetteville Trail (#5) and Kaymoor Trail (#8) (GPS: Lat. 38.05950, Long. -81.08051).

Wolf Creek Falls is below the road and a little downstream from the trailhead parking. Walking downhill on the outside edge of the switchback, you'll notice a few indistinct paths dropping down to the creek. These will lead to Wolf Creek Falls. Be forewarned, the descent is steep, rocky, and choked with rhododendron. Wolf Creek Falls has a picturesque drop, massive boulders at the bottom, and a lovely, emerald-green plunge pool. Wolf Creek Falls is truly a hidden treasure of the New River Gorge. But then, there are many other such jewels in the gorge. So if you have a taste for adventure and discovery, head for the New River Gorge.

Happy Trails!

CHAPTER 7

Hiking the High and Low Roads In the New River Gorge

"You take the high road and I'll take the low road, And I'll be in Scotland afore ye." That's an oft quoted lyric from an old Scottish tune called the *Bonnie Banks O' Loch Lomond*. It implies that the low road is better. That might be true in Scotland, but when it comes to hiking in the New River Gorge, both the high AND low roads are great ways to explore the sights, especially the cliffs of the Endless Wall.

The Endless Wall Trail

By "high road" I mean hiking trails that run along the top of the great sandstone cliffs that form the rim of the New River Gorge. "The Endless Wall Trail" maintained by the National Park Service is a good example. You can pick up this trail from either of two trailheads on the Lansing-Edmond road. The Fern Creek parking area (GPS: Lat. 38.06298, Long. -81.05682) is at a dip in the road about 1.25 miles from its junction with U.S. 19. Although a lot of rock climbers stop here in order to access the great climbing routes from Fern Point to Diamond Point, there's generally plenty of parking for hikers, too. The trail follows Fern Creek for about a half a mile. It's a gentle, forested trail that's a fine hike in its own right. At the half a mile mark, you cross Fern Creek on a nice foot bridge and begin a short ascent to the cliff tops. Upon reaching the top of the grade, you'll see a sign marking the Fern Point Overlook. Take this side trail for a fine view of the New River Gorge.

As you continue on the Endless Wall Trail, look for slightly worn paths to the right. These mark access points to other stony clearings and ledges that overlook the gorge. There are many such points, and all are worth your time, for each one gives you a different perspective of the New River Gorge as well as the massive sandstone cliffs that rim it. The cliffs range from 60 to 130 feet in height and are often sheer vertical to overhanging. The overlooks are unprotected in that there are no fences or ropes to prevent one from getting too close to the edge. So they aren't for small children or for those who are afraid of heights. But if heights don't bother you and you're careful, you can really see the gorge as few people do.

The Breathtaking Beauty of Diamond Point

Diamond Point is about 1/3 of a mile from Fern Point. In my mind, it's one of the premier viewpoints of the New River Gorge. I can honestly say that the view is breathtaking because the first time my wife Phyllis and I stepped out onto the rocky ledge overlooking the gorge, I gasped. The view literally took my breath away. I think you'll be impressed, too. Diamond Point juts out into the gorge like a promontory. It offers a sweeping, almost 270 degree panorama of the New River Gorge. It's a great place to sit and admire the handiwork of the mighty New River, which at this point has carved a canyon nearly 1000 feet deep. It's also a great lunch spot, so pack a sandwich or two. My wife and I always do. I can't explain it, but a peanut butter and jelly sandwich at Diamond Point always tastes a whole lot better than one at our kitchen table.

After savoring the view at Diamond Point, I'm sure there'll be a bounce in your step on the mile or so return trip to the trailhead. And if this hike whets your appetite for the cliffs of the New River Gorge as much as it did mine, then let me suggest another hike that includes the best of both worlds–the high AND low road around the New

River Gorge cliffs. Indeed, this hike has a bit of adventure to it. It requires blazing trails off the beaten path, descending a ladder to the base of the Endless Wall, and finding what I call the "Secret Passage" back to the top of the cliffs.

This hike begins at the second trailhead of the Endless Wall Trail (GPS: Lat. 38.05982, Long. -81.04953), which is just a half a mile beyond the first trailhead on the Lansing-Edmond road. For the first half a mile, the trail follows a small stream, crests a ridge, and then slopes gently downhill to a trail junction. At the junction bear left and after just a few yards note a trail spur to the right. Before descending this spur trail, check out the rock outcrop just ahead. It's a wonderful overlook with a great view of Diamond Point, which stands out at the end of the cliff line. After you've soaked in the scenery, take the spur trail. It leads down a cleft in the rocks and deposits you at the top of a wooden ladder leaning against a short cliff face.

Take a Ladder Down the Cliffs!

This ladder, called the Miner's Ladder, is one of three that have been constructed along the Endless Wall Trail to provide rock climbers with access to the base of the cliffs. The Fern Point Ladder is just below the Fern Creek Buttress, and the Honeymooner's Ladder is just northeast of Diamond Point and provides access to the middle of the cliff line. My wife and I became interested in the climbing ladders the first time we took the Endless Wall Trail. From the top, we spotted hikers walking along the base of the cliffs below. It looked like fun, but we weren't about to lower a rope and rappel down the cliff to get to the bottom. Inquiring at the Canyon Rim Visitor Center, we learned about the climbing ladders. The kind lady at the information desk gave us a National Park Service brochure titled "Climber Information," which mapped out climbing access trails and ladders. She then looked at my gray hair, what's left of it that is, and gently tried to discourage us from taking the ladders. Well, we've done all three ladders and can tell you from experience that the Miner's Ladder is the easiest. I wouldn't recommend the other two to people our age. I'll be 60 this year and my wife's age is, well, let's just say she's a little younger than I am. But we can still do the Miner's Ladder, and that's why I'm recommending this hike.

Peering down from the top of the Miner's Ladder is a bit intimidating to us non-climbers, but it's a sturdy fixture. It's made of solid wood and is securely fastened to the cliff. On the way down last time, I counted 19 2x4 rungs spaced about 15″ apart. That makes the ladder about 24 feet high. The ladder descends into a broad, open cleft in the rock face. At the bottom of the ladder, it's a somewhat steep, but not dangerous descent to the cliff base.

The Low Road at the Cliff Base

At the bottom, bear left and make your way along the trail that follows the foot of the cliffs. Now you're on the "Low Road." This path will give you another view, from below, of the impressive cliffs of the New River Gorge. The way isn't an improved or marked trail, but rather a beaten path forged by climbers and hikers. You have to pick your way along the foot of the cliffs, which is easy in most places. Don't worry about getting lost! The cliffs are always in sight and are towering reminders of where you've been and which direction to go. Just follow the cliffs.

Believe me, watching the cliffs will not be a problem. They are spectacular. As you exit the cleft at the base of the Miner's Ladder and turn left (east), you'll be passing under some cliffs named "The Cirque" by rock climbers. Here the cliffs of the New River Gorge form a massive, vertical to overhanging wall more than 120 feet high. It's a gorgeous sight if you'll pardon the pun. The sandstone rocks of the cliff face have been etched and sculptured by the slow but sure hand of Nature and in many places are exquisitely stained in multiple tones of brown and red by the gentle brush strokes of weathering. I marvel at these rugged yet artful displays every time I see them. I would rather walk these sandstone walls any day than the halls of some fine art museum.

If you hike along the base of the cliffs for about a half a mile, you'll come to a dirt road. It might seem like more than a half a mile because the path along the cliff base is a scramble in places and will seem longer than a leisurely stroll on an even trail. Turn left on the road. This road, which follows Short Creek, gradually ascends out of the gorge and eventually leads back to the Lansing-Edmond road. The hike back to the parking lot and the trailhead on the hardtop road is about a mile and a half. But there's a way back to the starting point that's more interesting and lots more fun.

The "Secret Passage"

Instead of taking the road back to the trailhead, I suggest looking for what I call the "Secret Passage" to the top of the cliffs, which is an easy and convenient way to ascend the cliffs. There's no ladder to climb, and the way is not steep. My wife and I stumbled on this passage way several years ago while exploring the cliffs from above. To locate the passage, which is not at all obvious from the dirt road, look for a trail taking off to the right that descends into Short Creek. It'll be marked as a climbing access trail. Don't take this trail, but instead continue for about 40 steps or about 100 feet up the road. Look to your left for a slight break in the cliff line. There'll be a couple of trees in front of the break and a tabular boulder leaning to the left against the left side of the cleft. The boulder obscures what is a nice open cleft in the cliff wall, which will take you to the top without too much trouble. The toughest part is getting around the boulder blocking the passage.

Once on top and on the "high road" again, turn left and follow the path worn by hikers and climbers. This path is easy to trace in some places and more difficult in others. But as in the case of following the low road below, the cliff line is always there to help you keep your bearings. As long as you don't wander too far away from the cliffs, you'll find your way back to the trail at the top of the Miner's Ladder.

On the way back along the top, I recommend scouting some of the spur trails that lead straight out to the gorge. They will generally take you to rocky outcrops with great overlooks of the canyon of the

New River. One such overlook is at the point where the trail crosses a power line clearing. It's not long after you've made the ascent up the secret passage. The side trail diverges to the left at the clearing and offers an open view of Beauty Mountain, Keeney Creek, and the rapids of the New River. Another rocky ledge closer to the Miner's Ladder, provides a splendid overview of the New River Gorge, Diamond Point, and the colorful sandstone cliffs of the Cirque.

Once back at the Miner's Ladder, just retrace your steps on the trail back to the parking lot and trailhead. And congratulations! You've just toured the cliffs of the New River Gorge on the high and low roads!

CHAPTER 8

The Most Beautiful Mountain in Southern West Virginia

The most beautiful mountain in Southern West Virginia is appropriately named "Beauty Mountain." I realize that of all the lovely mountains that grace our fair state picking one above the others is quite impossible. But to me Beauty Mountain is the fairest of them all. When folks from out of state visit me and are looking for the best scenery that the New River has to offer, I take them to Beauty Mountain first. It showcases the New River Gorge like no other place. Beauty Mountain isn't really a mountain in the sense that it rises as a peak above the surrounding hills. Instead, Beauty Mountain is an unbroken stretch of sandstone cliffs running along the rim of the New River Gorge from Short Creek near Edmond, WV, to Keeney Creek. Nevertheless, the cliffs of Beauty Mountain tower more than 1000 feet above the New River. These lofty cliffs offer the best and most numerous overlooks of the New River Gorge of any place I've seen.

Let me describe a three mile round-trip trail around Beauty Mountain that will take you to these overlooks and, as a bonus, allow an up-close look at the cliffs themselves. The trailhead parking is along the Lansing-Edmond road, which is the first right off of U.S. 19 beyond the access road to the Canyon Rim Visitor Center. The parking area (GPS: Lat. 38.06022, Long. -81.03593) is about a mile and a quarter past the Diamond Point parking lot. Look for a small pull off to the left with a basketball goal. This pull-off will be opposite a road to the right with a sign for the Nuttall Cemetery. Park and walk this road to the right, called the Beauty Mountain Road (County Road 85/5), for about 600 feet until you come to a triple junction. There is limited parking here, too (GPS: Lat. 38.05862, Long. -81.03509). The right-hand road goes a short distance to the Nuttall Cemetery. The road to the left is the continuation of Beauty Mountain Road, on which you'll make the return trip. Take the center road, which gradually descends into the gorge. About a quarter mile beyond the triple junction, look on the left for a sign marking a trail for rock climbing access. Take this trail, which drops off the road and descends into a small gulch.

Become a Pathfinder

From this point you become, quite literally, a pathfinder. The trail you're taking isn't maintained or marked. It's an irregular path blazed by men and women who've been drawn to the rock faces and climbing routes of Beauty Mountain. I should add that my wife Phyllis and I have never gotten lost following in the footprints of these climbers. Indeed, they've led us to some spectacular sights that we would have otherwise missed. In fact, for hikers interested in exploring the New River Gorge National River, I recommend a rock climber's guidebook written by Steve Cater. It's in its third edition and is available online at Amazon and in the book section of Tamarack in Beckley.

The trail descends to Short Creek. Scramble your way across the creek and pick up the path on the other side. At this point, I found the way a little difficult to follow. Nevertheless, just keep working your way toward the cliffs, which should be straight ahead of you and a little uphill. As a rule of thumb, keep an eye out for the cliffs. They are unmistakable landmarks. You'll probably reach the cliffs where a power line crosses over them. Upon reaching the cliff, turn right, and follow the path that winds along the base.

Illustrated Geology

From here to the point where you'll ascend to the top of the cliffs, you'll pass more than 100 established rock climbing routes and will probably meet a climbing party or two. While walking the base of the cliffs, you're bound to be impressed by their size and beauty. Most of the cliffs are vertical to even overhanging walls from 45 to 150 feet high. The cliffs are composed of the Upper and Lower Nuttall Sandstones, as they are known by geologists, and are massive, light-brown to gray sandstones usually carrying an abundance of rounded quartz pebbles. According to geologists, the Nuttall Sandstones were deposited by ancient rivers more than 300 million years ago. The Lower Nuttall Sandstone stretches for miles up and down the Gauley River and Summersville Lake. Along the New River in Fayette County, the Lower Nuttall Sandstone combines with the Upper Nuttall to form the impressive 175 to 200 foot cliffs along the Endless Wall and Beauty Mountain. Ironically the remnants of those ancient rivers, namely the Nuttall Sandstones, now overlook the mighty New River.

If you look closely at the cliffs, you'll see evidence of the currents that deposited the sandstones. Cross-bedded strata are common and are indicative of river deposits. Layers of smooth quartz pebbles suggest that the current of the river was strong enough to round off these hard stones by tumbling and bouncing them along the river bed. Sometimes pieces of mud and clay fell into the ancient river sands. These rocks are softer and more easily eroded than the sandstone. They now form hollowed pockets and undercut ledges in the cliff walls. Indeed, if you've had a course in Geology, the walls of Beauty Mountain are an illustrated textbook of sandstone deposits.

Welcome to Beauty

As you hike along the trail at the cliff base, you'll pass the Burning Buttress and the Thunder Buttress. Both are colorful monoliths that boldly thrust themselves into the gorge. To me they are as finely and majestically formed as any sculpture of man. After about a half a mile, the trail will eventually lead to a major break in the cliff wall. At this point a small stream has cut a notch in the cliffs and offers a safe and easy way to hike to the top of the canyon rim. Keep the cliffs on your left and follow the trail that leads out of the gorge. The trail tops out at a clearing for a power line. Eventually you'll take the path to the right along the power line. But first find a well-worn trail that bends back to the left toward the cliff top edge. This path leads to a large, flat platform of sandstone at the cliff's edge that provides a perfect panorama of the New River Gorge. In my opinion, it's the best overlook of the gorge. From this overlook on the right, the rim rocks of the gorge stretch in an almost unbroken chain of cliffs culminating at Diamond Point. In front and some thousand feet beneath your feet, the New River rushes around a great horseshoe bend. To the left, Keeney Creek pours into the New River at a set of rugged rapids, and upstream the gorge disappears into the distance. This vista has it all. Rock climbers call this overlook "Welcome to Beauty," and that's exactly what it is.

But don't stop here. Continue on the trail that skirts the cliff top because two more vistas lie ahead. About 1000 feet beyond "Welcome to Beauty," you'll find another picturesque overlook at the Thunder Buttress. "Picturesque" is the right word, too. Steven Shaluta, Jr., a prominent photographer of West Virginia, published a dramatic photo of this rock outcrop in *New River: A Photographic Essay* by Arnout Hyde Jr. In addition, on a U.S. Geological Survey web site of archived photography you'll also find a picture taken from this spot by M. R. Campbell in 1899 (http://libraryphoto.cr.usgs.gov/). Obviously this overlook makes a great photograph, but it's better seen in person! If you're lucky, you might run into a group of novice climbers rappelling down the cliff here. Guides are known to take tour groups here for a taste of rock climbing. They're fun to watch and are as close as I'm going to get to the sport.

There's one more vista. So continue on the trail for a few more yards and look for a short spur to the left. It leads to a great view upstream of the New River Gorge that's nicely framed by evergreen boughs. And I can tell you from personal experience that it's a great place for a lunch break. From this point on, the trail quickly deteriorates into a nasty bushwhack with few open vistas. So I recommend backtracking to the power line clearing that was at the top of the trail ascending the cliffs. At the clearing go right and follow the trail under the power line. At the base of a steep incline in the trail, look for a level path on the right leading into the woods and take it. It's a great little bypass that avoids the ups and downs and broiling sun of the power line trail.

The Hall of Giants

Eventually the wooded path will rejoin the power line trail. Turn right and head down the power line. Near the bottom of a downhill stretch, take a path to the right heading back into the woods. You'll soon be engulfed in a maze-like setting of house-sized boulders. I call this place the "Hall of Giants." Exploring the halls between boulders is fun and will eventually lead to more canyon overlooks. One is on a large, flat, sunny platform of sandstone and the other is tucked under a shady overhang with a perfect bench to sit on made of gray shale. When you've thoroughly explored the Hall of Giants, scout out the trail that continues in the woods along the cliffs. After crossing a small creek, keep an eye out to the right for paths leading to rock outcrops. Along this section of trail the overlooks are too numerous to count, but each is worth your time.

This cliff side trail will eventually intersect the power line clearing again, and a few yards beyond, will end at a gravel road where there are a few pull offs for parking (GPS: Lat. 38.04592, Long. -81.02440). This is at a tee-junction. Taking the gravel road to the left will get you back to your car. The paved road in front heads back to Edmond, WV. But before returning, walk the gravel road to the right about 25 yards to the Beauty Mountain Overlook. It's as pretty as a picture, so take your camera. By the way, if you or those you are showing the sights to, aren't up for this somewhat strenuous three mile hike, you can always drive to this spot and park at one of the pull-offs.

Then walk back along the level cliff top trail and enjoy as many overlooks as you like.

To return to the trailhead parking, walk back on the gravel road. This is the Beauty Mountain Road and after a mile and a half walk, you'll find yourself back at your car. It's not a bad hike. The locals are friendly, and you'll get to see a little bit of rural Fayette County. And you'll have the satisfaction of circling the most beautiful mountain in Southern West Virginia.

Happy Trails!

Part Three

Summersville Lake: The Land Below "See" Level

"Between every two pines is a doorway to a new world."

John Muir in My First Summer in the Sierra (1911)

CHAPTER 9

Long Point: Doorway to a New World

One of my favorite quotes from John Muir is: "Between every two pines is a doorway to a new world." One trip to Long Point, and you'll agree. Long Point is a rugged promontory of sandstone that juts like a fortress into Summersville Lake, a 2800 acre impoundment in Nicholas County, West Virginia, just off U.S. Route 19. The lake is operated by the U. S. Army Corps of Engineers for flood control, recreation, and power generation. The lake is formed by a massive, rock-fill dam that straddles the steep canyon of the Gauley River. The dam is 390 feet high (about as tall as a 40-story building) and 2,280 feet long and is the second largest of its type in the eastern United States.

Recreation Around Summersville Lake

During weekends in September and October, water is released from the dam into the Gauley River to provide plenty of white water and rapids for rafters and kayakers. The lake level is eventually lowered to its winter pool elevation of 1,575 feet to provide maximum space for the storage of flood waters. During the early spring, beginning around April 1, the lake is allowed to rise about 80 feet to 1,652 feet above sea level. This level is maintained for summer recreation.

Summersville Lake is, indeed, a haven for all kinds of recreation. There's fishing, boating, bicycling, scuba diving and water skiing. In addition, there are two campgrounds, three boat launching sites, a marina, a swimming beach, a visitor center, six picnic areas, an archery range, and three hiking trails.

One of these hiking trails leads to Long Point. If you want to see where you're going before you get there, stop at the Long Point Overlook on Highway 129 (GPS: Lat. 38.21040, Long. -80.87435) just a mile and a half east of the dam. You'll get a great view of the blue-green waters of Summersville Lake and the rugged sandstone cliffs that hem it in. According to the West Virginia Geologic Survey, the cliffs are composed of the Lower Nuttall Sandstone, a massive, light-brown to gray sandstone usually carrying an abundance of rounded quartz pebbles. It's generally 75 to 110 feet thick and stretches for miles up and down the Gauley River and Summersville Lake. Along the New River in Fayette County, the Lower Nuttall Sandstone combines with the Upper Nuttall to form the impressive 175 to 200 foot cliffs such as the Endless Wall and Beauty Mountain that rim the gorge.

The Long Point Trail

The Long Point trailhead (GPS: Lat. 38.23387, Long. -80.86593) is located at an archery range near the Summersville Airport. Before you leave your vehicle, make sure you've packed a camera because you're going to be rewarded with a visual feast! It's an easy 1.8 miles hike out to Long Point. There are a few ups and downs, but for the most part the trail gently undulates through the forest. It follows an old road for about a half a mile before branching off along a broad ridge that progressively narrows as you approach Long Point. The Corps has placed signposts at half a mile intervals, so you can easily measure your progress. Just beyond the 1.5 mile marker, the trail cuts through a rhododendron thicket. Though it's difficult to see beyond the rhody, the ridge is narrowing, and you're getting closer to Long Point. At the trail's end a sign is posted saying: "Warning, Trail Ends Here." It doesn't. But it does mean that you have to be careful, for beyond the sign you'll be near sheer rock cliffs and open fissures in the rocks. Don't be put off by this. Just watch your step for the next 50 to 100 feet and you'll walk out onto the tip of Long Point. Now it's time to get your camera out. The promontory at Long Point once sat above a sweeping, horseshoe bend in the Gauley River. Now it stands as a castle surrounded by Summersville Lake. At the end of the point, you're treated to a nearly 360-degree panorama of sky, rock, and water.

A Doorway to a New World

At this point, you will have been well rewarded for your efforts, but quite frankly the best is ahead, and the real adventure lies between two pine trees just a few yards back on the trail. When you've soaked in all the scenery at Long Point, return to the sign marking the end of the trail. From the sign post pace off 150 steps along the trail away from the point. This should put you close to two small pine trees growing about a foot apart. Turn to the left and follow a "bush-wacked" trail–a path worn down by occasional hikers. It leads to a depression near the edge of the cliff.

Now here's where nature has been kind. The cliffs at Long Point are shear and steep, over 100′ high, and normally only rock climbers could scale down to the base of them. But to the left of the depression you'll find the head of a narrow cleft in the massive rock walls of the cliffs. This crevice is like an enclosed stairway which runs from the top of the cliff to the bottom. It's easy to negotiate and not a bit dangerous. In fact, the rock walls surround you as you descend.

You emerge from the crevice at the base of the cliffs. If you're visiting Long Point during the low water levels between November and April, then hold your breath because you're about to enter that "new world" that John Muir wrote of. Timing is everything here. During this period the lake is at low water and the scenery below lake level is revealed. I would also add a word of caution. Don't proceed if there's any snow or ice on the rocks. They're a challenge to negotiate as it is. But with ice it's downright hazardous. I find March to be the best time for this hike because the temperatures have warmed up. But don't wait till mid-April. By then the lake will be too high to walk around Long Point.

Moon Rocks!

As you emerge from the crevice, perhaps the first thing you'll notice are bold, beautiful, snow-white boulders of all shapes and sizes. The rocks are rough and angular and piled chaotically. It's like a scene from another planet or a lunar landscape. The rocks are brilliant white because they're below the water level during the summer and being submerged for so much of the year, they aren't stained by the oxidation and weathering of iron-bearing minerals. So the rocks are in their most pristine state.

You'll also notice tree stumps poking up between the boulders. The stumps were left when the Corps cleared the slopes of the lake in the early 1960's prior to filling it. Since all the soil has been winnowed away by the waters of the lake, the roots of the trees have been laid bare and resemble the arms of an octopus. The textures of the tree stumps are fascinating, too. The bark is gone, but the wood beneath is not rotten. Rather it's dried, cracked, and desiccated and either chocolate brown or silver gray in color. A cluster of these old tree stumps looks like a "phantom forest."

In some ways, the environment below the water level at the lake resembles something out of the desert southwest. The rocks are bare and craggy, and the vegetation is sparse. If you didn't know better, you might think you were in Arizona or New Mexico. It truly is a new world.

A Temple of Stone

Even though the terrain is rough and rocky, with care you can walk through it. If you walk to the left (east), you'll catch your first glimpse of Long Point towering above you. Once you see it, you'll know why you packed the camera. Long Point is naturally photogenic. This dazzling promontory invites photography. As you make your way around the promontory, it changes character, presenting new facets, and seems to pose for pictures–all striking and inspiring. If you enjoy photography, you'll fall in love with Long Point.

After rounding the bend below Long Point, double back and explore the ground just below the point. You'll find arches, crevices, and a giant chamber enclosed by steep walls of stone. Once you've taken in all the scenery you can, make your way back to the cleft. You can't miss it. It's behind a huge pyramid of stone–a block of sandstone that's fallen from the cliffs and now lies on its side.

John Muir fell in love with Cathedral Peak in the Sierra Nevada Mountains of California. Among the glowing words he wrote about it were these: "From every point of view it shows marked individuality. It is a majestic temple of one stone, hewn from the living rock." Perhaps you'll feel the same about Long Point. I do.

And as for a new world waiting beyond two pines, I think John Muir was right–at least about Long Point. Give this hike a try, and see for yourself.

Happy Trails.

CHAPTER 10

Hiking the Shores of Summersville Lake: Satisfaction Guaranteed

Pirate's Cove, Cathedral Cave, and Orange-Oswald Wall. If it sounds like you're in for an interesting hike, you are! Waterfalls, caves, and cliffs are all part of the attractions of a hike along the shores of Summersville Lake in Nicholas County. But you won't find this trail on the official U.S. Army Corps of Engineers map. This trail is off the beaten path and has been blazed primarily by rock climbers drawn to the cliffs that border Summersville Lake.

The trailhead (GPS: Lat. 38.24603, Long. -80.85629) is just off U.S. Route 19 about a quarter mile north of the Hughes Ferry Bridge. Look for a parking area on the east side of Route 19. It's visible from the highway. Park your car. Lace up your boots, and by all means pack a camera because you're going to want it. The first time we hiked here, some rock climbers graciously led the way. I'm glad they did because the road to adventures along the lake is full of twists and turns.

The Way to Pirate's Cove

Near the end of the parking lot, take the road leading up to the top of the hill. At the crest of the hill, bear left and follow the road down a long rocky stretch. At the bottom of the hill, which is a half a mile from the trailhead, take a path that veers to the left and crosses a stream on an old log bridge. Just as you start climbing a rocky road, take a road that junctions to the right. Stay on the road till you come to another road junction and bear right again. Now you're on the road to adventure and scenic wonders.

After about a quarter mile, look for a broad way leading off to the right. You'll probably be able to catch a glimpse of the lake from here. If the lake is at high water, this is the only way into Pirate's Cove by land. Follow this broad trail down a gentle slope to a clearing near the edge of the cliffs overlooking the lake. You're sure to hear the sound of falling water, for you're right next to the waterfall at Pirate's Cove. You can catch a glimpse of the falls from the clearing, but there's a much better view to be had for those with a taste for adventure.

From the clearing follow a "bush-wacked" trail to the left that parallels the cliff. This will lead down to the edge of the cliff. Here nature and man have cooperated to provide a way down to the lake shore. For most of Pirate's Cove the lake washes against steep stone cliffs making access to the cove impossible by land. But just east of the waterfall, boulders have tumbled off the cliff and built a conical pile of rocks that stands above the lake level. That's what nature has provided. Now some kind souls have given nature and we non-rock climber types a hand. Two ropes hang in short runs down a sloping, rocky outcrop of about 15 feet in height. Don't be intimidated by this description. You're not going to be dangling by a rope to the side of a cliff. The ropes just help you maintain your balance and footing and help ease you down the rock outcrop. So give them a try. And remember this rock scrambling tip: Up is easier than down! Trying to pick your way down a slope is always more difficult than scaling up it. So if you can go down a slope you can be sure you can go back up it. You won't get stranded at Pirate's Cove!

Once on the rock island work your way to the shore for a fantastic view of Pirate's Cove and its waterfall. Watch for a wink from the waterfall because it's so picturesque that it begs to have its picture taken. The falls drop freely about 40 feet into the blue-green waters of Summersville Lake.

Walk the "Planks": The Ladder to the Cliff Base

When you've soaked in the scenery, taken your share of photos, and are ready for more adventure, return to the ropes at the apex of the rock pile and scale the rock outcrop back to the top. Back track to the main road and turn right. Continue about a fifth of a mile and then look for a well-worn trail breaking off to the right. Follow it down to the creek bed and then walk along a stream-side trail to the top of a cliff and another surprise—actually two surprises—another waterfall flanked by a wooden ladder leading to the bottom of the cliff. The ladder is sturdy, well-anchored to the rock cliff, and isn't high. There are ten sturdy rungs, and the descent isn't more than 15 feet. And you'll have the waterfall beside you all the way. By the way, a hearty "thank-you" to the rock climbers who built the ladder for forging a way to the bottom for us lesser mortals to traverse!

The ladder deposits you at the base of the cliff. Take the trail for about 50 feet to a junction. Your options at this point depend upon the time of year. At low water levels (November to March) you can take the right-hand fork and work around the base of the cliffs all the way to Pirate's Cove. The scenery during low water is breathtaking.

Cruise the Rock Climbing Cliffs

For the time being we'll assume that Summersville Lake is at high water for summer and fall recreation. In this case bear left at the trail junction and follow a well-worn path that hugs the base of the cliffs. The lake will be on your right and the cliffs are on your left. As you skirt the sheer rock cliffs and promontories, keep your head up because you're bound to spot rock climbers scaling the rock walls. All of the climbing routes have names, such as, Maximum Over Drive, Spice, Smilin' Jack, Souled Out, and No Bolts About It.

Vertical joints and horizontal bedding planes have carved the sandstone cliffs into unique and spectacular forms. You'll see dazzling overhangs, sheer rock faces, and long vertical fissures. In addition, the weathering of iron-bearing minerals in the sandstone paint the rock with a palette of dark red, brown, and orange highlights. One such weathered wall is called Orange-Oswald by rock climbers. You'll have no problem spotting it, but for your information it's about 3/10 of a mile from the base of the ladder.

On to Cathedral Cave

Beyond Orange-Oswald the trail becomes a little more rugged because rock climbing routes thin out and fewer people venture beyond. But do continue, because there's a scenic pot of gold at the end of this trail. Past Orange-Oswald you'll come across some overhangs and ledges in the cliffs—a great spot for lunch if you packed some sandwiches. Perched on the ledge you can see the lake while the overhang shades your picnic.

When you're ready to press on the trail, you'll cross a small stream that knifes through a notch in the rocky crags. A little further and you'll encounter a narrow cleft in the cliff wall. A large vertical joint in the sandstone has allowed a piece of the cliff to slip away forming a narrow fissure about 10 feet high and just wide enough to walk through. On a hot summer day a walk through the fissure is a nice break from the heat because it's always a cool 55 degrees in the cleft.

Continue hiking until you come to a field of huge boulders strewn at the base of the cliffs. Exploring different routes through this tangle of rock is like negotiating a maze. After exiting the maze you'll discover a little-known natural wonder, a cave that sits opposite the confluence of the Hominy River and Summersville Lake.

This cave is more like a Gothic cathedral. Indeed, that's why I call it Cathedral Cave. It's about 15 feet wide and 50 feet high. The rock walls taper steeply to an apex that runs the length of the cave. The cave is not only high; it's 120 feet long and open at both ends. The walls are decorated with green algae and a red-brown mosaic of iron-staining.

You can walk the length of the cave and exit at the opposite end and continue on the trail. But if you've had enough adventure for one day, you can retrace your steps. It's a relatively easy hike, a little less than two miles, back to the parking lot. At a leisurely pace you can make the return trip in just about an hour.

I forgot to mention that the name of one of the climbing routes along the trail is called, "Satisfaction Guaranteed." When you reach the parking lot, I hope you'll feel that way about the whole hike.

Happy trails!

CHAPTER 11

Whippoorwill: A Wild Beauty

I shall never forget the first time my wife Phyllis and I visited Whippoorwill. We were driving north on U.S. 19 approaching the bridge, which crosses Summersville Lake. Our guidebook for rock climbing routes said to watch for Whippoorwill Road on the left (west) side of the highway (GPS: Lat. 38.23220, Long. -80.85063) just before the bridge. The guidebook promised awesome cliffs along the lake below Whippoorwill and even a waterfall, all of which we were eager to explore. We saw the road sign and shifted over to the left-hand lane. While checking my rearview mirror before changing lanes, I noticed that a dark-blue pickup truck about a hundred yards behind us was also shifting into the left lane. When we pulled into the turn lane in the highway divider, the blue pickup followed us into the turn lane. I crossed the southbound lanes, and turned onto Whippoorwill Road. The blue pickup turned left, crossed the southbound lanes, and turned onto Whippoorwill Road. I made a quick jog to the right and continued. The blue pickup made a quick jog to the right and continued. Now as far as I know, no one lives on Whippoorwill Road. There are no visible houses, no driveways, no mailboxes, and no signs of habitation anywhere. Dedicated in September, 2012, there is a memorial cemetery off Whippoorwill Road holding the graves of 41 black workers who died from silicosis after working in the Hawks Nest Tunnel in the early 1930s.

Nevertheless, we followed the road for about 800 feet to an abrupt dead end in the woods. The blue pickup followed us right into the dead end and stopped behind us. Now at this point I felt that there were two possible options. We were either going to get mugged or meet some rock climbers. Fortunately, it was the latter. We met a nice young family—mom, dad, a little seven or eight year-old daughter and a tan colored dog. They had driven all the way from Virginia that morning to go rock climbing at Whippoorwill and, as fate would have it, arrived at the turn off at the exact moment we did. We chatted briefly, exchanged notes about finding the trail down to Summersville Lake, watched the little girl put on a backpack, and saw them take off for the lake. We followed in a few minutes.

Easy Access

By the time we reached the lake, dad was already halfway up a cliff face, and the little girl was playing with her dog, which illustrates why I prefer Whippoorwill when exploring Summersville Lake at low water. The access is easy. At Long Point you have to hike 1.75 miles just to reach the lake shore. At Pirate's Cove the trail is shorter, but it's hilly. At Whippoorwill, you simply walk a few yards up from the dead end, walk a level, dirt road toward the lake for about 500 feet, and then drop down a steep, but not treacherous gully to the cliff base. Indeed, the young family that we met proved to me that if you're eight years old or older and have four legs or two, you can reach the base of the cliffs without much effort.

But there's much more to Whippoorwill than easy access. The area showcases the hauntingly beautiful and mysterious land below "see level" around Summersville Lake. I'm referring to the terrain around the shores of Summersville Lake at low water levels. During the spring and summer, the U.S. Army Corps of Engineers, which manages Summersville Lake, keeps the lake level high, about 1652 feet in elevation, for recreation. During the fall, the water level is lowered about 75 feet to its winter pool elevation of 1575 feet. As the water recedes, a terrain emerges that I find otherworldly and absolutely captivating.

I suppose the first things that catch your eyes are the tree stumps. Before Summersville Lake was filled, the trees below lake level were cleared, leaving a veritable forest of tree stumps behind. But these aren't ordinary looking stumps. A typical stump looks like a gray-brown octopus that has been frozen in place. Tree roots radiate from the stump like tentacles and wrap boulders in strangleholds. The roots are visible because the lake waters have winnowed away all the soil. If you can imagine a typical wooded mountainside stripped of all soil and loose material such that all the underlying rocks are laid bare, you have an idea of the terrain around Summersville Lake at low water.

A Forest Frozen in Time

In some ways it's a land frozen in time. The lake was completed in 1966, at this writing some 41 years ago. Yet the wooden stumps and roots have not decayed or deteriorated. How is this possible? As it turns out, the waters of Summersville Lake have not rotted the stumps; instead, they've preserved them. Wood decomposes most readily, either organically or chemically, in the presence of oxygen, light and warmth. But none of these are abundant in Summersville Lake. The waters of the lake are naturally cold, and sunlight cannot penetrate much below 15 feet in depth. And although there's enough oxygen in the water to keep fish alive, there's not enough to promote the decomposition of wood. Because of these factors, logs can be preserved underwater for hundreds of years.

Indeed, a whole new industry, the salvaging of underwater logs, is developing in Canada. A company called Logs End harvests logs from the Ottawa River that sank in the heyday of logging operations in the 19th Century. These logs are milled and used as beams, flooring, and paneling in homes today. Triton Logging of Vancouver, British Columbia, developed and manufactures a remotely controlled submersible called the "Sawfish," which is the world's only deep water logging machine. In many reservoirs worldwide, trees within the lake limits were left standing. Most salvage loggers believe these reservoirs conceal 200 million to 300 million trees in submerged forests worldwide. One look at Summersville Lake at low water, and this staggering fact seems believable.

The Land Below "See" Level

Rocks as well as logs are preserved by the lake. Some rocks are thinly covered with brown silt that settles upon the rocks as the lake level lowers each year. On the other hand, many of the rocks are as white as freshly fallen snow. I like to call them "moon rocks." The pure and natural color of the quartz-rich sandstone rocks, which is white, is also preserved by submersion. Lack of oxygen slows the decomposition of the iron-bearing minerals within the sandstones leaving them in their pristine white condition.

In some respects, the shores of Summersville Lake below the high water mark, the land below "see" level as I call it, is a land out of place. It lies among the lush green forests of West Virginia, yet resembles a parched desert. The rocks are rugged and bare; the trees are dry and desiccated, yet well preserved. The soil is thin or nonexistent. It's a stark and eerie landscape that I find hauntingly beautiful.

The Remnants of Ancient Rivers

But there's another side to the shores of Summersville Lake—the land above the high water level. And it has a charm of its own. Summersville Lake is rimmed by imposing vertical cliffs of sandstone, which West Virginia geologists in the early 1900s named the Lower Nuttall Sandstone. According to geologists, the Lower Nuttall Sandstone was deposited by ancient rivers more than 300 million years ago. If you look closely at the cliffs, you'll see a variety of textures in the rock that are common to river sands. Thick beds of sandstone with many parallel, horizontal layers are common. But you'll also observe beds of sandstone where the layers are slightly tilted from the horizontal, yet are still parallel to one another. These are called cross-bedded strata and are commonly associated with river deposits. Smooth quartz pebbles imbedded in the sandstone suggest that the current of the ancient rivers was strong enough to round off these hard stones by tumbling and bouncing them along the riverbed. Sometimes pieces of mud and clay fell into the ancient river sands. These rocks are softer and more easily eroded than the sandstone. They now form hollowed pockets and undercut ledges in the cliff walls.

The Artistry of Whippoorwill

To add to the artistry of these richly textured sandstone walls, many are coated in hues of red, brown, black, and yellow. The earth-tone colors are created by weathering, in this case, the oxidation of iron-bearing minerals within the sandstones. When fresh, these iron minerals, such as pyrite, magnetite, and pyroxene, are generally dark in color. They are few in number compared to the white and clear grains of quartz and are dispersed throughout the sandstone or confined to distinct layers. In either case, they do not contribute much color to the sandstone. But when these iron minerals come in contact with water, oxygen, carbon dioxide, or organic acids, they break down into other minerals such as hematite, goethite, and limonite. These minerals create a palette of earth tones. Hematite, derived from a Greek word meaning "blood" because of its red color, occurs in a soft, fine-grained, earthy form called red ochre. Goethite and limonite are similar in composition and are brown-black to yellow and are called yellow ochre. In ancient Greece the term "ochre" was used for natural earth pigments. The most dramatic use of ochre is found in the cave paintings of prehistoric man found in France, Spain and North Africa.

At Summersville Lake, nature is the artist and the sandstone cliffs her canvas. Exquisite patterns, textures and hues of red, brown, and yellow ochre adorn the cliffs creating a giant, outdoor mural of fine art. To me these painted cliffs are masterpieces to be relished and admired. I never tire of them.

But there's more. Indeed, Summersville Lake is home to a host of artistic riches. In addition to natural paintings, sculptures embellish the shores. The cliffs have been carved by the slow but sure hands of time and gravity. The shoreline is strewn with angular rocks, boulders, and monoliths of all shapes and dimensions. Like chips hewn by some giant chisel, the rocks lie in chaotic heaps below the sandstone cliffs. They remain where they fall, and yet some seem posed by an unseen hand. My favorites are the pyramid-shaped stones that pose majestically against the sky. Nevertheless, these fallen boulders are but the chips. The cliffs are the statues cut in stone. Many of the cliff walls are perfectly planar and vertical as if cut swiftly by a sharp blow. Other cliffs defy gravity with massive overhangs. Still others resemble rectangular blocks stacked one upon the other.

Nature's Chisel

The chisel that carved the cliffs has a name. It's a geologic term called "joints." A joint is a rock fracture, or break, along which no movement has occurred. Most regions have at least two sets of joints, which are generally at right angles to each other. The dominant set, called systematic joints, is the most pervasive. They are usually vertical and cross cut other joints. Non-systematic joints are not as well developed and do not generally cross other joints. On the Appalachian Plateau, where most of West Virginia is located, the systematic joints are oriented northwest, while the non-systematic joints trend northeast. Joints are also planes of weakness. Water percolates along joints, which speeds weathering and erosion. Over time, narrow joints can grow into wide fissures and become zones of weakness, which can rupture.

Since the two joint sets are vertical, at right angles to each other, and are zones of rupture, they, in effect, dice the sandstone layers into rectangular blocks. Looking at the cliffs along Summersville Lake, it's easy to see how the joints have shaped these stone walls. Long, linear cliff lines run parallel to a joint set. The cliff lines are abruptly interrupted by rectangular blocks that jut out from the cliff face at a perpendicular angle. These blocks are aligned with the opposing joint set. Large rectangular blocks fall from the cliffs when the rock ruptures along both sets of joints. Once aware of this process, you'll notice it not only at Summersville Lake, but on the Meadow River and New River cliffs, too.

So how can you best enjoy the artistry at Whippoorwill? After descending the trail to the cliff face, turning right (north) will take you to a waterfall. Since it's fed by an intermittent stream, the falls will be filled with water only in the spring or after a heavy rainfall. Nevertheless, it's worth the effort to see. The northern route, however, offers only a half a mile or so of cliffs to explore. On the other hand, the cliffs south of the trail stretch on for a mile or more. Heading south I'd advise hugging the cliff wall as much as possible. You'll see all the features that I've described here and no doubt make discoveries of your own. One last tip. If the lake level is low, you can return to the cliff access trail on a dirt road that runs along the water's edge. Not only does it offer a different perspective of the cliffs and dead tree stumps, it's level and flat and a lot easier than hiking among the rocks close to the cliffs. Your legs will love you for it.

Beauty is Where You Find It

My wife and I are continually amazed by the beauty of West Virginia. Truly you don't have to venture far to find nature at her best. It's tucked here and there in enchanting corners of West Virginia. These words of John Muir could easily fit those blest to live in the Mountain State: "To the sane and free, it will hardly seem necessary to cross the continent in search of wild beauty, however easy the way, for they find it in abundance wherever they chance to be."

Whippoorwill is one such place of wild beauty.

Part Four

The Potomac Highlands

"Climb the mountains and get their good tidings. Nature's peace will flow into you as sunshine flows into trees. The winds will blow their own freshness into you, and the storms their energy, while cares will drop off like autumn leaves."

John Muir in Our National Parks (1901)

CHAPTER 12

Following in the Footsteps of Frontiersmen: Rediscovering the North Fork of the Blackwater River

"Perhaps in all this broad land of ours, whose wonders are not yet half revealed, no scene more beautifully grand ever broke on the eye of poet or painter, historian or forester. The Blackwater here evidently breaks its way sheer down through one of the ribs of the backbone of the Alleganies. The chasm through which the river forces itself thus headlong tumultuous down, is just wide enough to contain the actual breadth of the stream. On either side, the mountains rise up, almost a perpendicular ascent, to the height of some six hundred feet. They are covered down their sides, to the very edge of the river, with the noblest of firs and hemlocks . . ."

An Expedition Into the Wilds of Canaan

Philip Pendleton Kennedy penned those words in 1852 in a colorful account called *The Blackwater Chronicle: A Narrative of and Expedition into the Land of Canaan*. And who could blame him for waxing poetic. He was leading a party of fellow adventurers into a raw and relatively unexplored region of West Virginia–Canaan Valley and the upper watershed of the Blackwater River. The explorers were lured by the keeper of the Tower's Inn in Gormania who boasted: "Gentlemen, if you can only reach the fall of the Blackwater, you can take more trout in an hour than you ever took before in all your lives." That did not prove to be an exaggeration. Kennedy and his company caught native trout, which had never before seen a baited hook, by the hundreds.

The wilds of Canaan, however, did not easily yield their treasures. These men sloshed through dank swamps and slashed through dense laurel thickets. The going was tough, but the rewards were grand. Kennedy's party had crossed Backbone Mountain and were descending the North Fork of the Blackwater River when they came upon an inspiring scene. Kennedy breathlessly described it this way:

> Turning a rocky promontory that jutted the mountain side, the Blackwater, some hundred yards ahead, seemed to have disappeared entirely from the face of the earth, leaving nothing visible down the chasm through which it vanished, but the tops of fir-trees and hemlocks . . . The expedition stepped out upon the furthest verge and very pinnacle of the foaming battlements, and gazed upon the sight so wondrous and so wild, thus presented to their astonished eyes.

They were approaching the brink of what is now called Douglas Falls–the point at which the North Fork of the Blackwater River begins its precipitous descent into the Main Fork. Further discoveries lay ahead as chronicled by Kennedy in his book.

Is There Any Adventure Left?

But is there any adventure left for us in the Land of Canaan some 150 years later? Can we follow in the footsteps of these explorers and experience the wonder they felt? The answer is, "Yes!" If you're lodging at Blackwater Falls State Park or in surrounding areas and are willing to stay a few more days, then I suggest you spend some time exploring the North Fork of the Blackwater River. It's only four miles from the state park. If you do, you'll get a taste of adventure and discover for yourself some scenic gems that few people have seen since Kennedy and his men forged the way in 1852.

An excursion on the North Fork should start at Douglas Falls. Beginning from the entrance to Blackwater Falls State Park at State Route 32, drive about two miles north on Route 32 until you come to the Douglas-Coketon Road on your left. After leaving Route 32, drive about a mile to a bridge crossing the North Fork. Immediately after the bridge look for a gravel road to the left, which is an abandoned railroad grade that runs for 10 miles along the length of the North and Main Forks of the Blackwater River all the way from Thomas to Hendricks. It's a great bike path. Up to Douglas Falls, it's also passable by vehicle. But I wouldn't try it with my sedan. It has some deep potholes that require a vehicle with high clearance.

Douglas Falls

Since Douglas Falls (GPS: Lat. 39.12403, Long. -79.51965) is just a mile down the road and the way is fairly level, you can hike, bike, or drive it pretty easily. On the way keep your eye out for some abandoned coke ovens on your left. One look at the structures and you'll know why they were called "beehive" coke ovens. The way is strewn with wildflowers, too, and occasional glimpses of the North Fork of the Blackwater. Although this is a fairly flat stretch, the river does make a couple of short leaps and runs over sandstone ledges.

When you reach a Forest Service gate across the road, the falls will be immediately to your left. Take the path that leads down to the falls and explore them. Douglas Falls are not as high or as wide as the Great Falls of the Main Fork of the Blackwater, but they are picturesque and beautiful nonetheless. In fact I find them stunning.

The falls drop some 40 feet into an emerald plunge pool surrounded by huge prisms of rusty-red sandstone. The rocks are tinted red by iron-bearing minerals leached from acid mine drainage upstream. The coal mines have since been reclaimed, but the boulders are colorful reminders of the past pollution.

A Mysterious Second Waterfall

Though the falls of Douglas are striking and dramatic, there are many more falls on the North Fork as it makes its descent into the Blackwater Canyon. Indeed, an intriguing entry in Kennedy's Blackwater Chronicle led me to look for one of them. In Kennedy's description of his scramble down the North Fork below Douglas Falls, he wrote: "This level of the stream, however . . . leads you to a second large fall, a clear pitch again of some forty feet." When I read that, my eyes widened. A second large fall as high as Douglas? I had neither read of these falls in any modern travel guides nor seen photographs of them. Was Kennedy exaggerating–merely caught up in the thrall of the cascades?

I had to find out, and the only way to do so was to follow in his footsteps. With the help of some kayakers who ran the North Fork, I found the falls. I'll call them Kennedy Falls after Philip Pendleton Kennedy, the man who first wrote of them.

Kennedy Falls

To find Kennedy Falls (GPS approximate: Lat. 39.12033, Long. -79.52036) continue down the railroad grade along the North Fork. Scrambling along the stream bed is difficult at best and somewhat dangerous. If you read Kennedy's account, you'll know what I mean. It's much better to parallel the stream along the road and then descend straight into the canyon at the point of the falls. Hiking about a quarter mile below Douglas Falls should put you at the point of descent into the canyon. If you come to a rock cairn composed of sandstone cobbles, you've gone too far. The falls are indeed directly downslope from the cairn, but there's an easier way down the side of the canyon. Backtrack about 86 paces or 215 feet to find the best point of entry into the woods.

Descend into the canyon at this point and head straight down the slope. But use caution. The slope is very steep. Fortunately the way is fairly clear, and you don't have to do much "bushwhacking." When you reach the bottom of the canyon, you should be near the falls. Bear right and downstream a little to reach the head of the falls. You can scramble around the falls on the right to see them from below. The falls are about 30 feet high and lovely indeed. A rocky gravel bar in the middle of the stream provides a great frontal view. The levels above the falls beg for attention, too. The rocks are red like those at Douglas Falls and finely sculpted by the river.

Aside from some intrepid kayakers, I don't believe many people have seen these falls. When viewing them, you could be standing right in the foot prints of Kennedy and his fellow explorers.

One of the Best Blackwater Canyon Overlooks

To be sure, there's more to explore along the course of the North Fork, but if you're yearning for some wide open vistas, backtrack to the Douglas-Coketon road and turn left. When you reach the end of the pavement, park on the graveled turn outs to the right or left. The road continues up Backbone Mountain as Forest Service Road 18 and is passable with a high clearance four-wheel drive vehicle. From there hike up the road about one mile. Look for a sharp curve to the right at a point where a dirt road takes off uphill to the right (GPS: Lat. 39.11464, Long. -79.52442). Explore the left shoulder of the forest service road for trails leading down into the woods. Follow these trails for about a thousand feet. They're fairly easy as "bushwhacking" goes and will lead you to a small set of cliffs jutting into Blackwater Canyon. These rock outcrops give you a great panorama of the Blackwater Canyon as it makes a sweeping horseshoe bend. It also overlooks the confluence of the North and Main Forks of the Blackwater River. In my opinion, it's one of the best viewpoints you'll find of the Blackwater Canyon. It's a great place to relish this still rugged and wild land.

Walking in the Footsteps of Frontiersmen

As you turn back for cabin or camp or cottage having walked in the footsteps of these frontiersmen, perhaps you'll feel as Kennedy did when he finished his first day exploring the North Fork:

The sun broke out, and we proceeded on our way up the steep ascent–rainbow over-arching the waterfalls, and the spray everywhere golden with sunbeams. At length, reaching the top of the grand chasm, and standing again on the brink of the impending rocks where we first hailed so rapturously, the leap-down of the river–we took a last look of the wild scene and went on our way to the camp.

CHAPTER 13

The Canaan Valley National Wildlife Refuge: A Feast for the Eyes and a Refuge for the Soul

Several years ago, my wife, Phyllis, and I packed the kids in the car and went in search of autumn beauty. For two days we toured West Virginia from north to south, and we were rewarded with some gorgeous scenery. Yet, as we were returning home, we discovered that the most glorious foliage of all was along the lane approaching our own little house! There was beauty in our own backyard, yet we had failed to appreciate it.

I became acquainted with this truth yet again last fall. For the last 10 years, our family has rented a cabin for a week at Blackwater Falls State Park, always spending time hiking and photographing the deep woods, rugged cliffs, and picturesque waterfalls of the Blackwater Canyon. We also explored the highlands of Dolly Sods, the Flat Rock Plains, and North Fork Mountain, paying little attention to the lowlands and valleys of the area. But last year, instead of heading for our usual haunts in the highlands, Phyllis and I explored the trails and scenery of the Canaan Valley National Wildlife Refuge (GPS of Visitor Center: Lat. 39.04506, Long. -79.44585). There we discovered a feast for the eyes and a refuge for the soul. We found a treasure trove we had overlooked for years—a remarkable place we had driven by many times but had never really seen.

Magic on the Middle Valley Trail

Thanks to refurbished access roads and 31 miles of designated trails, we spent six days hiking and photographing in the refuge. It was a revelation. The wetlands, grasslands, and forests mesmerized us with their charm. While hiking the Middle Valley Trail off of A-frame road (Trailhead GPS: Lat. 39.09667, Long. 79.36317), we happened upon a field of cotton grass and ferns. The ferns were decked in fall hues of orange, yellow, and brown, while the white puffs of cotton grass hovered weightlessly around and above the ferns. It was sheer magic. For a few precious moments, we both felt like Alice stepping through the looking glass into Wonderland. Earlier in the week, along the Middle Valley Trail, we were dazzled by fields of goldenrod. In the warm, afternoon sun, swarms of monarch butterflies danced from flower to flower. Magic again. I photographed the monarchs to my heart's content. On the Beall Trail off of Courtland Road (Trailhead GPS: Lat. 39.06361, Long. -79.41805), wildflowers of all varieties and hues lay at our feet. Though we are novices at wildflower identification, in just one afternoon on this trail we identified well over a dozen. There were many more that escaped our untrained eyes, but, nonetheless, they created a showcase of floral splendor that we will never forget.

Later, for a taste of the high country and its sweeping vistas, we took the Valley Overlook Trail (GPS: Lat. 39.13560, Long. - 79.33287). After a short but steep hike, we were treated to some spectacular panoramas of the northern end of Canaan Valley. What a grand place indeed. In six short days, the Canaan Valley National Wildlife Refuge had won our hearts.

An Ecological Treasure

As early as the 1950s, biologists from WVDNR and the U.S. Fish and Wildlife Service recognized the uniqueness of Canaan Valley to both West Virginia and to the eastern United States. Sitting about 3,200 feet above sea level and covering 32,000 acres, Canaan Valley is the largest high-elevation valley east of the Rockies. Nestled in the valley floor is one of the largest shrub swamp environments in the East. Canaan Valley also holds the largest wetland complex in West Virginia, containing about 9,500 acres of bogs, shrub swamps, and wet meadows.

These unique environs are home to a staggering diversity of plant and animal life. According to the U.S. Fish and Wildlife Service the area supports more than 40 distinct plant communities, with more than 580 species of plants. It is also home to an estimated 290 species of mammals, birds, reptiles, amphibians, and fish. But these numbers don't do the refuge justice. Where else in West Virginia could you see (depending upon the season) grebes, bitterns, herons, swans, geese, ducks, osprey, hawks, eagles, falcons, sandpipers, gulls, owls, hummingbirds, woodpeckers, flycatchers, vireos, swallows, and many other varieties of birds? If you're very lucky, you might even spot a loon, a cormorant, an egret, an ibis, a tern, or a lark. Though rare, these birds have been spotted in the refuge. The refuge also provides an important habitat for eastern migratory birds. The Blackwater River, which meanders slowly through Canaan Valley, is home to more than 20 species of fish, including darters, minnows, dace, suckers, and bass, as well as both native and introduced trout. Mink, bear, bobcat, beaver, turkey, grouse, deer, raccoon, and squirrels also call Canaan Valley home, as do the endangered West Virginia northern flying squirrel and the threatened Cheat Mountain salamander.

The Uncertain Fate of Canaan Valley

Though the biologists who toured Canaan Valley in the 1950s recognized the treasure that the valley's wetlands, grasslands, and forests represented, for the next 40 years, the fate of the Canaan Valley wetlands was very much in doubt. While federal and state agencies and conservation groups worked to preserve them, Monongahela Power Company submitted plans to build a hydroelectric storage facility that would have flooded much of the valley's wetlands. Ultimately, a permit for the proposed hydro plant was denied by the U.S. Army Corps of Engineers. The matter was contested in court, however, and wasn't settled until the power company lost its final appeal in 1988.

With the acquisition of 86 acres in 1994, the U.S. Fish and Wildlife Service established the Canaan Valley National Wildlife Refuge "to preserve its unique wetlands and to protect the fish and wildlife resources of the valley." With this acquisition, Canaan Valley became the nation's 500th wildlife refuge. By 2002, the refuge had grown to about 3,300 acres. On February 14 of that year, lovers of Canaan Valley got a huge valentine when Allegheny Energy Inc., Sen. Robert C. Byrd, Rep. Alan Mollohan, and others announced the sale of 12,000 acres in the northern part of the valley to the U.S. Fish and Wildlife Service. Today, the Canaan Valley National Wildlife Refuge encompasses about 16,550 acres.

As a general policy, the U.S. Fish and Wildlife Service encourages wildlife-depended recreation in six different forms: 1) nature observation, 2) photography, 3) hunting, 4) fishing, 5) environmental education, and 6) interpretative programs. You can enjoy all of these activities in the Canaan Valley National Wildlife Refuge. According to the refuge Web site, the following game species can be taken on refuge lands during applicable seasons: white-tailed deer, black bear, wild turkey, ruffed grouse, mourning dove, waterfowl, coot, rail, gallinule, snipe, woodcock, rabbit, hare, squirrel, red fox, grey fox, raccoon, bobcat, woodchuck, coyote, opossum, and striped skunk. All other species of wildlife are protected. Hunters must carry a current, signed Canaan Valley Refuge hunting permit; the appropriate state hunting license; and a photo ID.

"The Property of Unknown Generations"

The importance of the Canaan Valley National Wildlife Refuge is perhaps best captured by the words of President Theodore Roosevelt, whose vision led to the founding of the national wildlife refuge system: "Wild beasts and birds are by right not the property merely of the people who are alive today, but the property of unknown generations, whose belongings we have no right to squander." To be sure, Canaan

Valley is not just a state treasure, it's a national treasure-an inheritance that must be conserved.

One good way that concerned citizens can contribute to the future welfare of the refuge is to support The Friends of the 500th, a nonprofit citizens group founded in 1996 to preserve and enhance the refuge. Among other activities, The Friends host bird watching, plant and animal observation, and photography sessions; offer human and natural history programs; plan and conduct special projects on the refuge; and try to foster an understanding of the importance of balancing the needs of humans and wildlife. Contact by mail at P.O. Box 422, Davis, WV 26260. For more information about this and other matters concerning the refuge, visit www.fws.gov/refuge/canaan_valley/.

Thanks to those who recognized its worth and to those who continue to work for its conservation, the natural jewel that is the Canaan Valley National Wildlife Refuge will be preserved for succeeding generations to treasure and enjoy.

CHAPTER 14

Nature as Sculptor: Rock Art at Dolly Sods

One clear fall day, my wife, Phyllis, and I were hiking the open heath of Dolly Sods, miles from civilization. Suddenly, out of the corner of my eye, I caught the figure of a man with bulging biceps. He looked rock solid and squarely built. He stood frozen, his massive legs rooted in the ground. For just a split second I wondered, "Have I caught a glimpse of Big Foot or a Sasquatch, or maybe the Lost Backpacker of the Potomac Highlands?" But a second glance told me no. Instead, the imposing figure was one of the fantastic forms carved in the stone outcrops along the high ridges of Dolly Sods. Perhaps my mistake was forgivable. The rocks that rim Dolly Sods have been sculpted into exquisite forms that truly resemble everything from humans and animals to abstract art. Carved by the slow but sure hand of nature for more than 100,000 years, these rock sculptures stand today as ancient works of art.

Sitting atop the Potomac Highlands of Tucker, Randolph, and Grant counties, Dolly Sods is a high-elevation, upland plateau covering about 20,000 acres. It's famous for its rocky plains, bogs, flag-form spruce, and sweeping vistas. The 17,000-acre Dolly Sods Wilderness Area has been set aside for backpackers and overnight hikers. Since my wife, Phyllis, and I are strictly day hikers, we enjoy exploring the 2,000-acre Dolly Sods Scenic Area, which runs along the eastern edge of the Dolly Sods plateau and parallels Forest

Road 75 (FR75). Fortunately, the Scenic Area is prime territory for locating the rocky sculptures that line the eastern rim of Dolly Sods.

Bear Rocks

Located at the northern end of FR75, Bear Rocks (GPS: Lat. 39.06611, Long. -79.30154) is a great place to whet your appetite for the rock art of the Sods. Bear Rocks is a rugged exposure of a rock formation geologists call the Pottsville Conglomerate. Deposited more than 300 million years ago, when the Appalachian Mountains were much taller than they are today, the Pottsville Conglomerate is composed of sandstone containing layers of rounded, white quartz pebbles. These hard sandstones and conglomerates run the length of the eastern and western ridges of Dolly Sods.

At Bear Rocks weathering, that is the disintegration and decomposition of rock surfaces, has carved the Pottsville Conglomerate into some fascinating forms. Perhaps the most notable is what some photographers call the "Dragon of Dolly Sods." This creature has a round, protruding head, eyes, a mouth, and what appear to be wings. To find the Dragon take the footpaths from the parking area to the "Bear Rocks Preserve" sign constructed by the Nature Conservancy. Facing the sign, take a heading in the direction of about 2 o'clock. The Dragon is among some taller rocks that sit about 30 yards off the edge of the ridge.

The dragon and other striking stone shapes at Bear Rocks introduce you to the rock sculptures of the highlands, but even more interesting art awaits further south along the eastern rim of Dolly Sods. In the fall of 2007, as we drove on FS75 on the last day of our vacation, Phyllis spotted some prominent rock outcrops on the eastern rim just north of the Red Creek Campground. We vowed to return and explore them, and the next year, on the first day of our fall vacation, we did just that. On FS75, at the end of a stand of pines about 0.3 miles north of the Red Creek Campground, we found a parking area and the beginnings of an unmarked trail leading toward the eastern ridge. For about 600 feet the trail was easy to follow. But when it led into some waist- to shoulder-high shrubs, the pathway broke down. Beyond this area a maze of deer trails took us to the eastern rim.

Camel Rock

Upon reaching the ridge, we hiked toward the prominent outcrops that Phyllis spotted the year before, which were about a quarter mile north of us. On reaching the outcrop, we discovered a cornucopia of shaped rocks. Here sub horizontal layers, also called bedding planes, of the Pottsville Conglomerate tilt about 5 to 10 degrees to the west. The outcrop is also sliced by vertical fractures into large, rectangular prisms of stones with rounded edges, the highest being about 10 feet tall. Vertical surfaces are carved into troughs and ridges resembling corrugated cardboard. The horizontal surfaces of the rocks are pitted with rounded depressions of varying diameters and depths. These depressions are called weathering pits or gnammas (nam-uhs), the latter a term borrowed from the Aborigines of Australia, who depend on the water trapped in natural rock bowls for survival. These bowls, ridges, and vertical breaks combine to give the stone surprising shapes. At this particular outcrop, I saw the profile of a camel, so I dubbed it "Camel Rock."

Here nature's handiwork reminded me of an art appreciation course I took in college. The class visited an art museum in downtown Los Angeles and was assigned to study and write an essay on a sculpture by Henry Moore, a British abstract, organic sculptor. The piece, called "Reclining Figure," consisted of three large, sub rounded and disconnected forms. Back then, I thought that sculpture was limited to works resembling Michelangelo's "David," and I couldn't comprehend Moore's abstract shapes. But over the years, I've grown to appreciate abstract forms and their ability to stimulate the imagination and evoke diverse responses. Without revealing any more of my ignorance of art, suffice it to say that the rock sculptures of Dolly Sods resemble the works of Henry Moore more than Michelangelo.

Nature's Hammer and Chisel

After spending an afternoon crawling over and photographing this outcrop, I began to think more about how such shapes were formed. Since I have a degree in Geology, I applied the principles I'd learned to discern some of the sculpting tools of nature. I believe that weathering is both hammer and chisel in the hands of nature. Physical weathering is the mechanical breaking of rock. A form of physical weathering prevalent at Dolly Sods is frost wedging, which happens when water enters a pore or crack in a rock and freezes. Water expands as it freezes, widening the cracks or pores and often loosening or dislodging rock fragments. Wherever water can seep into solid rock, whether it is a small opening, such as between two grains of sand, or a large opening, such as between a crack or fracture, it can, by expanding into ice, apply enough force to break the rock. Chemical weathering is the breakdown of a rock surface through chemical processes such as oxidation, solution, and hydrolysis. Chemical changes to a rock can soften it and make it more susceptible to being washed away. Rock can even be dissolved and carried away by water. Weathering, then, is the process that wears down the hard rock outcrops of Dolly Sods.

If physical and chemical weathering are the hammer and chisel of nature, then differential weathering is the artist. Differential weathering accentuates subtle variations in a rock's composition and structure. Gnammas, for instance, are examples of differential weathering. Should just a slight rock weakness cause a small depression to form on a horizontal rock surface, water, seeking the lowest spot, will preferentially flow into it. Should the temperature drop below freezing, the water will turn to ice, expand, and break up the rock particles next to it, making the small depression just a little larger. The enlarged depression will attract more water, which, when turned to ice, will further expand the hole. In this way the process feeds on itself, and after repeated cycles of freezing and thawing, what was once a small depression will have grown into a full-fledged gnamma. Gnammas deepen and expand outward, which eventually limits their growth. If the outer circle of a gnamma reaches the edge of a boulder or rock outcrop, the bowl will be partially breached. Further expansion carves a larger breach in the side of the bowl. Eventually the bowl is destroyed leaving, U-shaped openings and rounded columns, exactly the shapes forming the camel's "head."

The Hands of Time

Geologic studies show that gnammas can take thousands to tens of thousands of years to form. A study of gnammas in Portugal by David Dominguez-Villar and others showed that, in general, the relative age of gnammas was best indicated not by width or even volume but by depth ratios. Without getting more technical, we can say that generally, the deeper the gnamma, the older it is.

Indeed, time is another key factor in nature's sculpting of rocks. Dr. Greg Hancock, Professor of Geology at the College of William & Mary, has studied the age of the outcrops on the east and west rims of Dolly Sods. He found that these rocks have been exposed at the surface for 60,000 to 240,000 years. That means that differential weathering has been gradually picking away at them for tens and even hundreds of millennia. Above all, time is a fine hand. Over millennia, every subtle weakness in the rock, each small variation in rock composition, and even the slightest difference in natural openings are delicately but persistently magnified and accentuated. In the hands of time, weathering is a powerful tool, having carved the rocks of Dolly Sods into the intricate forms we see today.

Crystal Ship and Keepers of the Heath

North of Camel Rock there are other stone sculptures on the eastern rim, including ones I fondly call the "Crystal Ship" and "Keepers of the Heath." To get to the Crystal Ship, Phyllis and I parked at the Beaver Dam Trailhead on FR75 (GPS: Lat. 39.05304, Long. -79.30947), about one mile south of Bear Rocks. On the east side of FR75, opposite the Beaver Dam Trail, there's a faintly worn but distinguishable foot path heading east. We followed this path through the brush, down a rocky ledge, through more brush, and then to an open bog. Rock cairns marked our path across the bog to another rocky ledge. Once past the second rock ledge, we made our way to the eastern rim. The distance from the road to the rim is only a third of a mile, but because of the uneven terrain, it felt longer to us. Once at the rim, to our left (north, that is) we caught sight of a tall and mysterious looking rock topped by what appeared to be a large, stone wing. After photographing this winged rock from many angles, I felt it resembled a sailing ship. Since it is composed of hard, crystalline sandstone, I christened it the "Crystal Ship." Good art stirs emotions, and I confess that the sight of Crystal Ship uplifts and inspires me as much as any work created by man.

The gnammas on top of this outcrop are deep–a sure sign of age. The wing is a hard, weather-resistant layer of sandstone that has been left suspended by the removal of less sturdy rock beneath it. The rock rises some 15 feet above the heath and sits on a gentle knoll. Its height, relative to the surrounding heath, reflects the processes of differential weathering, too. In geologic terms, this tall outcrop is called a high or a tor, the latter a word derived from a Celtic word for hill or tower.

Dr. Hancock explains that tors are also formed by differential erosion. Elemental in this process, in this case, are natural vertical fractures called joints, which control the location and development of tors. Being open cracks in rock, they collect water. Frost wedging breaks the rock along the joints, making the joints wider and deeper. Since joints in rock are not evenly spaced, zones of more tightly spaced joints will be broken up at a faster rate than zones of widely spaced joints. These zones of tightly spaced joints will break up and be washed away more quickly than adjacent areas, thus developing shallow troughs called lows. In like manner, tors will form where fractures are not as numerous as in surrounding areas. This aspect of differential weathering builds on itself, too. As highs form, water runs off of them and into the lows, further increasing the activity of frost wedging. Over time, differential weathering causes the lows to become lower, thus making the tors stand out higher. So, in addition to its deep gnammas, the relative height of the Crystal Ship above the surrounding heath suggests that the hands of nature have worked this rock for many millennia.

Exploring the Crystal Ship led Phyllis and me to discover yet another tor on the eastern rim. Just a quarter mile south of the Crystal Ship, two large stones stand shoulder to shoulder, keeping watch over the heath, and thus the name "Keepers of the Heath." This is where we discovered the stone statue that I called the Lost Backpacker of the Potomac Highlands at the beginning of this chapter. At Keepers of the Heath, the forces of differential weathering are again illustrated. For example, the Keepers tor sits between and above shallow lows. The "backs" of the Keepers are pockmarked with gnammas, but the gnammas are small. Since the rock face containing these gnammas tilts at about 45 degrees, the gnammas could not have held water in this position. The base of the Keepers must have been undercut, causing the rocks to eventually tip to one side. Even more tors lie between the Keepers and Camel Rock. They've been exquisitely carved over many millennia by the very slow but exacting hand of nature. They're just waiting to be explored, interpreted, and, above all, appreciated.

Happy trails!

CHAPTER 15

Germany Valley Overlook Cabins
Rustic Luxury

Stepping for the first time into Cabin 1 at Germany Valley Overlook Cabins was a moment my wife Phyllis and I will cherish. We had just spent a glorious afternoon hiking a trail that runs along the crest of North Fork Mountain in Pendleton County. Called by some the best trail in West Virginia, it did not disappoint. From the trail in the distance to the west, Spruce Mountain stretched across the entire horizon from north to south. In front and below Spruce Mountain ran the hog backs and rounded hills of the Fore Knobs. And directly below us lay the lush pastures of Germany Valley. Returning to the trailhead on U.S. 33 about nine miles west of Franklin, WV, we drove just a half a mile to the entrance of Germany Valley Overlook Cabins (GPS: Lat. 38.70722, Long. -79.41194) and quickly arrived at Cabin 1. It was unlocked and ready for our arrival. As we crossed the threshold of the cabin, we immediately realized that we had left behind the scenic mountain trail, but not the vistas or the views. To our delight, the view out of our cabin windows was as pleasing as the mountaintop trail. Spruce Mountain still loomed in the west, the foreground hills were closer and just as lovely, and Germany Valley spread out before us as though it were our very own playground. The term "picture window" assumed real meaning as every cabin window offered a vista that was as pretty as a picture. We discovered firsthand that at

Germany Valley Overlook Cabins we could enjoy the best of both worlds–the beauty of the great outdoors in the comfort of a cozy cabin.

Deluxe Accommodations

Indeed, the cabins offer a number of ways for vacationers and travelers to enjoy the best of both worlds. For instance, the Germany Valley Overlook Cabins are uniquely constructed, blending deluxe accommodations with rustic construction. As I sat in the cabin scanning the interior, I coined the phrase "rustic luxury." To me it made sense and described the cabin perfectly. Tenderly and lovingly built in 2005 and 2006 by the owners and operators Bill and Luci Raines, all three cabins are very well kept. They come with all the comforts of home including a fully-equipped kitchen, appliances, and a full bath with a shower. The furnishings are tastefully selected. There's electric heat and depending upon the cabin a gas fireplace or a wood burning stove. The extras reveal the personal touch of Bill and Luci who obviously anticipated the needs of the families and friends that would share these cabins. Picnic tables, Adirondack chairs, fire pits (with axe and wood provided!), charcoal grills, full-length porches–the Raines have provided all the accessories for a thoroughly enjoyable cabin stay. As nice as it is to spend time in a rural cabin, I never felt as though we were "roughing it." On the contrary, I had the pleasant notion of feeling pampered by the comfortable accommodations thoughtfully provided by Bill and Luci.

Rustic Charm

While accommodations of the Germany Valley Overlook Cabins are first class, they are not overly modern or sterile. Being log cabins, they are rustic by nature and by construction. The interiors are entirely of wood. Exposed wooden beams and logs crisscross the cabins supporting vaulted ceilings while hardwoods cover the floors. And all of the cabins are different, each with a unique floor plan and construction. Cabin 1 was assembled from logs from a neighbor's small sawmill about four miles from the cabin. Bill and Luci designed and built this cabin inside and out from plans Luci sketched on graph paper. As the smallest cabin, it covers 900 square feet and sleeps a maximum of six. Cabins 2 and 3 are kit cabins from BPB log homes. Bill and Luci built the outer structures and designed the interiors to their liking with local materials. For instance, Cabin 2 features a peeled cherry log staircase railing. The cherry logs came from the Raines' farm, and were hand-peeled by them. The interior walls of Cabin 3 were made from lumber salvaged from an old house that was going to be torn down. The wood on the walls is white walnut, knotty pine, and bull pine. Cabin 2 is the largest with 1400 square feet and sleeps a maximum of nine. Cabin 3 has 954 square feet and is wheelchair accessible. For all of the items mentioned above, I like the term "rustic luxury" for the cabins at Germany Valley, where you can enjoy some of the niceties of a luxury resort and yet savor uniquely constructed log cabins that exude rustic charm.

The Lookout Cottage

The newest addition to Germany Valley Overlook Cabins only adds to the uniqueness of the lodging. Built in 2014 on a portion of the property called "Picnic Ridge," Cabin 4 is appropriately named the Lookout Cottage. It's a two story structure designed and built by the Raines to resemble a fire tower, and it functions like one, too. Sitting on the highest portion of the property and sporting a covered deck surrounding the second story on three sides, the Lookout Cottage is tailor made for soaking up the panoramas of pastoral Germany Valley. It sleeps up to six lucky people.

Secluded But Not Isolated

There is yet another way to savor the best of both worlds at the Germany Valley Overlook Cabins, and that is to enjoy the serenity of seclusion without feeling isolated. Space and lots of it surrounds every Germany Valley Overlook Cabin. The rental cabins sit on about equal portions of 170 acres of pasture and grazing land. Each cabin is private. There are no other cabins or structures nearby. There are no thoroughfares, no cars or trucks parading to and fro in front of your cabin. All you see is nature and so much of it. Beyond the cabin porch lies an expansive view of one of the most picturesque places in West Virginia–Germany Valley. Tucked behind the hog back ridges of the Fore Knobs and overshadowed by the towering escarpment of North Fork Mountain, Germany Valley is a secluded paradise of rolling pasture lands and forest groves where the peace is palpable.

Recreation Opportunities Nearby

This type of seclusion often comes with a price–isolation, but not in this case. If you can tear yourself away from the view through the picture window, if you have the will power to lay aside that book that you've just discovered time to read, or if you have the wherewithal to set down that freshly brewed cup of coffee, then there are plenty of things to do and places to go that are just minutes from the cabin. Phyllis and I generally use a cabin as a base camp from which to explore the surrounding points of interest. After a hearty day of hiking, the comfort of knowing that a cozy cabin, instead of a long drive, awaits you is unbeatable. As I mentioned at the beginning of this chapter, before Phyllis and I checked into our cabin, we hiked the trail along the crest of North Fork Mountain. The distance from the cabin to the trailhead couldn't have been more than a mile. But that's not all. Seneca Rocks, a prominent West Virginia landmark, is just 15 miles west on U.S. 33. By the way, I suggest that you hike the trail to the top of Seneca Rocks. To be sure, the vertical change in elevation is a thousand feet, but the trail is in my opinion one of the most evenly graded trails in West Virginia. The Nelson Rock Preserve, a unique private outdoor recreation spot for the whole family, is just four miles west on U.S. 33. The steep rock escarpments of Nelson Rock Preserve offer amateurs some of the trappings of rock climbing in a safe environment. If you prefer a guided tour of underground limestone caverns, Seneca Caverns is a little more than six miles away, and Smoke Hole Caverns is about 28 miles. If fishing sounds like fun, you can wet a line at the Buckhorn Trout Farm in Fort Seybert, WV, about 22 miles from the Germany Valley Cabins.

What's more the Potomac Eagle Scenic Railroad, featuring a three-hour train trip into the heart of the eastern home of the American Bald Eagle, is no more than a 45 minute drive. A little further out, say within an hour's drive, are some of my favorite places: the Dolly Sods Wilderness and Backcountry Areas, Canaan Valley, Blackwater State Park, the Smoke Hole Recreation Area, and Spruce Knob (the highest point in West Virginia). And should you seek the amenities of the city such as a bank ATM, groceries, restaurants, etc., the town of Franklin, WV, is just 10 miles from the cabins. In addition, if you'd like a break from the kitchen, home cooked meals are served at the Gateway Restaurant in nearby Riverton, just seven miles west on U.S. 33.

Rich in History

This isn't an exhaustive list of nearby recreation sites. Depending upon your interests there are also many places to explore for arts, crafts, and points of historical importance. This includes Germany Valley whose history dates back to 1761 when John Jacob and Maria Magdelena Hinkle migrated with their 12 children and their families from North Carolina to settle in Germany Valley. Actually, Bill and Luci Raines are part of the rich history of Germany Valley. Bill Raines is a direct descendent of the Hinkle's that originally settled the valley, and Luci's family settled in nearby Circleville in the early 1700s. They now own and manage the Cabins and a farm in Germany Valley. (For more information on the history of Germany Valley, please refer to an article written by Dr. Kenneth H. Carvell in the September 2000 issue of *Wonderful West Virginia*).

The Best of Both Worlds

The Germany Valley Overlook Cabins have much to offer travelers and vacationers: Modern, deluxe accommodations in rustic log cabins, glorious views of the great outdoors from the comforts of a cabin, and the serenity of seclusion coupled with easy access to a variety of West Virginia's finest recreational opportunities. Perhaps the character of these cabins is best captured by the entries left in the Guest Book–another evidence of the personal touch that Bill and Luci Raines have built into their cabins. "We were greatly renewed by the peace and beauty of this place" (J.B. of North Carolina). "The beautiful view and secluded nature of this spot brought us here and will bring us back" (L.A. of Baltimore, MD).

I couldn't say it any better. The Germany Valley Overlook Cabins in Pendleton County are worth experiencing for yourself. In so many ways, they offer you the best of both worlds.

Part Five

Rivers Wild and Wonderful

"Who publishes the sheet-music of the winds or the music of water written in river-lines?

John Muir in Wild Wool (1875)

CHAPTER 16

Adventures on the Gauley River: No Raft? No Problem!

You strap on your helmet, cinch down your life jacket, grab a paddle, clutch your raft, bolster your courage one more time, and push off into the Gauley River for the ride of your life. Many folks will be doing just that as the whitewater rafting season begins this fall on the Gauley River. But what about those who prefer to stay ashore? Are there any adventures on the Gauley for landlubbers? Sure there are and plenty of them! They're not the same as wielding an oar through whitewater, but they are fresh and exciting nonetheless. If you're up for walking a perfectly straight line in nearly perfect darkness for 2/3 of a mile, if you're ready to walk across the Gauley River from 60 feet above its surface, if you're able to scramble down to a little known waterfall with a good 40-foot drop, then you're ready for some adventures on the Gauley that don't require a raft.

Laurel Creek Falls

Gauley River adventures began for me a few years ago when my wife, Phyllis, and I spent a couple of nights at Hawks Nest Lodge to celebrate our 35th wedding anniversary. Being hikers, we were looking for new places to explore. An acquaintance of mine recommended Laurel Creek Falls (GPS: Lat. 38.21430, Long. -81.02950), which he had uncovered on one of his waterfall hunting expeditions. He kindly gave me directions to the waterfall, which I will pass on to you.

But first a word of advice. Though the base is firm, the gravel road to the falls has some mud holes, rocky high spots, and is very steep at the end. An SUV or four-wheel drive truck is much better suited for this road than the family sedan. To find Laurel Creek Falls, from the intersection of U.S. 19 and U.S. 60, take U.S. 60 4.6 miles west to Saturday Road. From Hawks Nest Lodge go east on U.S. 60 for 3.25 miles. Saturday Road is at the town of Hopewell and runs northeasterly from U.S. 60. It's a paved road that weaves through some lovely pastures and forests. After 5.5 miles, take a sharp turn to the left onto Lucas Road. Continue for one mile. At a sharp turn to the left at the crest of a hill, continue straight onto a gravel road. This road follows Laurel Creek to the Gauley River. When you come to junctions in this road choose the direction that trends downward and follows the creek. Two miles on this gravel road will take you by a wooden shelter on the left below some sandstone cliffs. Stop here. You're at Laurel Creek Falls!

As a waterfall photographer, Laurel Creek Falls has all the photogenic elements that I appreciate in waterfalls: A free drop over a sandstone ledge, a bold staircase of cascades, and a quiet pool at the base. In addition, the falls are beautifully framed by trees and rhododendron around the sides and emerald-green, moss-covered boulders at its base. The falls are easily viewed from the top; however, the scramble to the base of the falls is steep and rocky. I generally walk about 25 yards down the road from the wooden shelter and carefully descend the slope down to the creek. Below the falls, Laurel Creek leaps over several small rock ledges forming a striking series of cataracts.

The Tunnel

Gauley River adventures don't end at Laurel Creek Falls. The falls roughly mark the boundary of the Gauley River National Recreation Area, and more outdoor excitement lies ahead. Continuing 0.2 miles on the road takes you down to the shores of the Gauley River and to an abandoned railroad grade that runs along its banks. There's parking at the mouth of Laurel Creek and a large set of stairs leading to the river's edge used by rafters to reach the shores of the Gauley.

The abandoned roadbed is a remnant of a twenty-eight-mile stretch of railway built by the NF&G (Nicholas, Fayette and Greenbrier Railroad Company) from 1929 to 1931 to connect the towns of Swiss and Nallen. Hiking this old railroad bed is an easy way to explore and appreciate many miles of the Gauley River. Two tunnels were built for this railroad–one about a mile upstream from Carnifex Ferry near the Confluence Resort, and the other is less than half a mile from the parking area at the mouth of Laurel Creek. To test your metal on this old tunnel, head downstream (west) on the railroad bed. The tunnel is straight as an arrow and about 0.6 miles long. From either end you can dimly see the proverbial "light at the end of the tunnel."

On the spur of the moment a couple of years ago, my son, Matt, and I decided to go to Laurel Creek and hike around at the Gauley River. We had hiked right to the face of the tunnel before either of us realized that we didn't have a flashlight. My son, bless his heart, wasn't going to let that stop him, so we tentatively entered the tunnel. With walking sticks we tapped the trail ahead of us hoping to avoid being swallowed up by a gaping mud hole. Matt took the lead guided by the faint light at the end of the tunnel. I bravely followed behind my son tracking the back of his jacket, which was ever so slightly illuminated by light from the tunnel entrance behind us.

We inched our way forward for the length of the tunnel and emerged at the opposite end without mishap. The dangers of the darkness never materialized. The tunnel trolls were politely absent. Bats didn't buzz us. And the ground did not swallow us up. In other words, it was just a little scary and a lot of fun.

Spanning the Gauley

I suppose if I had carefully studied my map before entering the tunnel, I wouldn't have been surprised by what greeted us as we emerged from the darkened passage into the light of day. But I hadn't, so I was! Within just a few yards of leaving the tunnel, the old rail line launches across the Gauley on a bridge spanning the river on concrete pillars some 60 feet tall. Crossing this bridge used to be daunting because the floor was composed of railroad ties with three to four inch gaps between each tie. This meant carefully gauging steps to miss the gaps between the ties while staring down between the ties to the water surface some 60 feet below–an act both troubling and titillating. Fortunately in 2009 the National Park Service built a new wooden floor with guardrails on both sides. Now bikes can be safely ridden across it. Suspended above the river, this old bridge presents sweeping panoramas of the Gauley both upstream and downstream as well as Peter's Creek, which empties into the Gauley, near the northwest end of the bridge. The bridge ends on the north bank of the Gauley River at an active railroad line. This is a good place to turn around and back track (pardon the pun). It's only 1.2 miles back to the Laurel Creek parking area where yet another adventure awaits.

Ramsey Branch Falls

Just one and a half a mile upstream from the mouth of Laurel Creek lies another spectacular waterfall at Ramsey Branch (GPS: Lat. 38.20100, Long. -81.01260). This waterfall sports a 40-foot free fall and is not difficult to get to. As a bonus, wildflowers adorn the road from Laurel Creek to Ramsey Branch. At various times of the year, Phyllis and I have noticed yellow sweet clover, spotted wintergreen, pale touch-me-not (jewelweed), pepper grass, spiderwort, yellow star grass, tassel-rue, thimbleweed, wine raspberry, St. John's wort, Japanese honeysuckle, phlox, along with many other blooms. At the junction of the old railroad bed and Ramsey Branch, two roads split off to the right. A rough, rocky road heads uphill and leads back to Saturday Road. The lower road drops down to the streambed of Ramsey

Branch. Take this road for just a few yards and stop at a hairpin turn at creek level. A short, bushwhacked trail leads upstream to the falls. At the falls, Ramsey Branch rolls over a sandstone ledge forming a broad veil of white water. Having photographed more than 70 waterfalls in the New River Gorge region, I believe that the falls at Ramsey Branch are one of the most picturesque. They are a "must see" for adventure seekers along the Gauley River.

To be sure, running the Gauley River in a raft is pure excitement, but the Gauley has more to offer outdoor enthusiasts than just whitewater. Within a couple miles of the mouth of Laurel Creek, you can soar on a bridge 60 feet above the Gauley River, explore a tunnel 400 feet beneath the mountains, and walk among 40-foot waterfalls. Looking for fun on the Gauley without a raft? No problem!

Happy Trails!

CHAPTER 17

The Falls of Hills Creek Scenic Area: The Story Behind the Scenery

Nestled in a narrow gorge off the flanks of Spruce Mountain in Pocahontas County lies a waterfall wonder called the Falls of Hills Creek (GPS: Lat. 38.17809, Long. 80.33861). Dashing down a steep course, Hills Creek descends over a series of three closely-spaced waterfalls of 25, 45, and 63 feet in height. Each waterfall basin is higher, wider, and more dazzling than the one preceding it. This outdoor spectacle culminates at a viewing platform in the midst of a broad, rock-hewn amphitheater showcasing the third waterfall. Taking a 63-foot free fall over a massive rock ledge, the third fall of Hills Creek is reported to be the second highest in West Virginia and is certainly one of the most picturesque. Yet all the beauty and splendor of the Falls of Hills Creek would be lost to us if it were not for nature's creative powers and man's desire to preserve and appreciate them. To me, the story of the Falls of Hills Creek Scenic Area illustrates nature and man working in tandem in unusual and creative ways.

The Creation of the Falls of Hills Creek

Along with fellow nature lovers, I appreciate the beauty of the land in its present form. Moreover, knowing geology allows me, with the mind's eye, to look into the past and interpret how landscapes have been modified by the process of erosion working over thousands of years. Indeed, according to the science of geology, the creation of the Falls of Hills Creek was both colorful and dramatic. Its birth is a story of "Piracy in the Highlands." Just as pirates on the high seas preyed upon passing vessels and stole their treasures, in the not so distant past, Hills Creek crept up upon the North Fork of the Cherry River and stole some of its waters. This geologic process is known as stream capture or stream piracy.

Thousands of years ago, Hills Creek was a small stream trickling off the southern flank of Spruce Mountain with little splash or fanfare. However, in time the headwaters of Hills Creek eroded upstream and into the path of the North Fork of the Cherry River. In doing so, from the point of intersection it robbed the Cherry River of its upstream flow. Thus all the run-off from Kennison Mountain that was pouring into the Cherry River above the point of intersection got diverted down Hills Creek. The watershed or catch-basin for the precipitation funneling into Hills Creek swelled from roughly 80 acres prior to the capture to 2800 acres afterwards. In proportion to its enlarged catch-basin, the volume of water flowing in Hills Creek swelled, too.

The shaded-relief map in this chapter provides a way to understand and visualize the stream capture. Perhaps the most notable evidence of a stream capture is the abrupt turn made by the present course of Hills Creek at its point of intersection with the North Fork of the Cherry River. From flowing due west out of its headwaters, Hills Creek makes a sharp left-hand turn to start flowing southeasterly. In addition, the ridge lines of Spruce Mountain and Point Mountain are clearly breached at Hills Creek. On the ground the best evidence for the stream capture is the pond on the north side of the Highland Scenic Highway (SR 39/55) at the turnoff to the Falls of Hills Creek Parking Area. A pond in the middle of what would normally be a free-flowing mountain stream is unusual. The pond marks the point of capture. Northwest of the pond, from a level, swampy area, the North Fork of the Cherry River sluggishly emerges to begin its course westward.

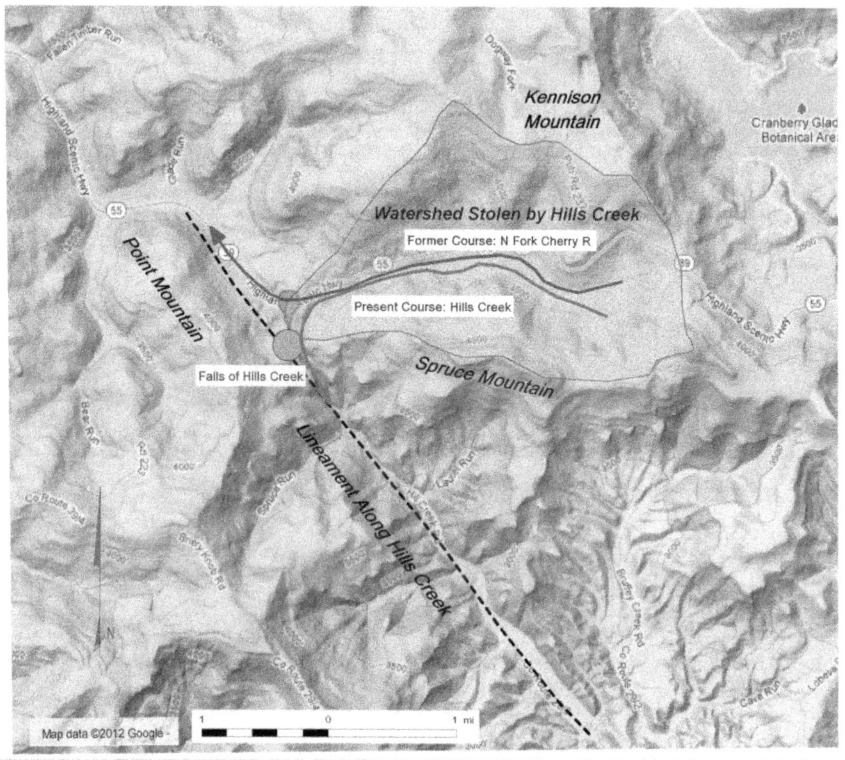

Shaded Relief Map of the Falls of Hills Creek

At the time of the stream capture, the three waterfalls of Hills Creek, as we know them today, were hardly more than bumps in the creek bed. However, the substantial increase in flow caused by the stream capture enabled Hills Creek to erode its streambed with greater vigor and speed. Hills Creek cut into and washed away the soft red and gray shales (finely laminated rock composed of layers of mud, clay and silt) along its course. But the gray sandstones (massively layered rocks composed primarily of individual grains of sand that have been cemented together), being harder than the shales, resisted erosion and washed away at a slower pace. Differences in the rates of erosion between shale and sandstone causes a geologic process called differential erosion. As the shales continued to erode, hard sandstone layers became the top ledges of waterfalls. Where shale underlies a sandstone ledge, the shale is prone to undercut the ledge causing a stream to plunge in an unbroken fall, as it does at the third waterfall on Hills Creek. After thousands of years of differential erosion along the course of Hills Creek, the three lovely waterfalls that we see today emerged.

The Hills Creek Lineament

Stream piracy is not the whole story behind the creation of the Falls of Hills Creek. In fact, the capture of the North Fork of the Cherry River by Hills Creek would probably not have occurred without another geologic feature–a lineament. By definition a lineament is a linear topographic feature of regional extent that is believed to reflect underlying earth structure. A lineament's simplest expression is a linear alignment of stream valleys shown on topographic maps, aerial photographs, or satellite imagery. Hills Creek is a prime example of such. Notice on the shaded relief map accompanying this chapter that Hills Creek runs southeasterly in a straight line for about four miles below the falls. Above the falls, the Cherry River runs northwesterly for one mile along the exact line. Lineaments are commonly composed of vertical fractures or breaks that are more numerous than the surrounding bedrock. These concentrated zones of breakage speed the weathering and erosion of the bedrock causing dips to form in the topography. These dips or low points naturally draw surface runoff and coalesce into stream beds. Thus, the comparatively weak rocks in the lineament on Hills Creek caused the creek to flow along the lineament. The softer rocks of the lineament also hastened the backwards retreat of the headwaters of Hills Creek and eventually led to its capture of the North Fork of the Cherry River.

The Forest Service Preserves and Perseveres

Hidden as they are in a gorge off the Highland Scenic Highway, the Falls of Hills Creek would go unnoticed by the general public if not for the efforts of the U.S. Forest Service (Forest Service) in West

Virginia. Prior to 1963, the route to the falls was roughed out by hardy hikers willing to battle slippery slopes, steep drop-offs, and dense rhododendrons. Perhaps no more than 100 people a year ventured down Hills Creek to see the falls. Recognizing the scenic value of the falls, in 1963 the Forest Service built a graded trail with many steps and a footbridge. With an improved trail in place, on October 1, 1964, the Monongahela National Forest designated a 114-acre tract as the Falls of Hills Creek Scenic Area.

But the Falls of Hills Creek story did not end there. In fact, it marked the beginning of a determined effort, and a struggle at times, by the Forest Service to keep the falls accessible to the general public. Geology again played an important role, this time by hindering access to the falls. As mentioned earlier, the bedrock at the Falls of Hills Creek is composed primarily of red and gray shales with occasional sandstone layers. Especially on steep slopes such as those found around Hills Creek, the shales are prone to slips and landslides. Furthermore, large trees find the footing difficult on the steep shale slopes and are prone to be toppled by wind and snow. Fallen trees and small slides have made the Falls of Hills Creek trail difficult to maintain.

A Chronology of the Scenic Area

In 1969, the trail was damaged by flooding. Nevertheless, in 1973 trail use had risen to about 10,000 visitors a year due in part to tours from the Cranberry Glades Visitor Center and nearby State parks. Despite Forest Service maintenance by manpower programs and YCC, the trail continued to deteriorate. In 1979, a slide took out the lower falls' observation platform and part of the trail. A new road and parking lot were built in 1980, but trail conditions continued to decline. In *Hiking the Mountain State*, author Allen de Hart referred to a "dangerous route" to the lower falls. By October, 1983, the trail to the lower falls had to be closed for public safety.

Undeterred, in 1986 personnel of the Monongahela National Forest Supervisor's office in Elkins and Gauley District Recreation

Assistant in Richwood called "for a bold, visually exciting new stairway of concrete or steel" to secure access to the lower falls. Jim McCoy, then a construction engineer and civil engineering technician for the Forest Service, oversaw the design and construction of the innovative trail system. In 1994 a new trail, bridge, and steel stairwell were opened to the public. Parts for the steel stairwell were flown in by helicopter and assembled on site. Nevertheless, the lumber (4x4's and 6x6's) and hardware (bolts, screws, nails, etc.) were all carried in by hand. In addition a 1700 foot long, four foot wide asphalt-paved accessible trail was constructed to the first falls. Artist renderings of the Middle and Lower falls were installed at the first falls' platform for those who could not continue the length of the trail. In 1998, accessible toilets were opened.

From 1999 to 2009 only basic maintenance was required to remove fallen trees and repair damage. However heavy snows during the winter of 2009-2010 felled numerous trees onto the boardwalk and contributed to a slide that took out 16 feet of boardwalk. The trail to the lower falls was closed again. However, by 2011 the Forest Service received special funding to repair the damaged boardwalk and stairs, and the trail to the lower falls was reopened.

The Falls of Hills Creek Today

Today the Falls of Hills Creek Scenic Area attracts approximately 30,000 visitors a year. Created by geologic processes some thousands of years ago and preserved by the Monongahela National Forest, today the Falls of Hills Creek Scenic Area can be safely appreciated by all nature lovers. The Forest Service's elaborate system of paved trails, natural pathways, boardwalks, wooden steps, a wooden bridge, a wooden staircase, a steel staircase, and five observation decks enable visitors to enjoy all three falls. The entire trail from the parking lot to the last observation deck at the third falls covers three-quarters of a mile and contains 382 steps. To preserve the Scenic Area for generations to come, treatments to its hemlock trees are ongoing to stop damage caused by the woolly adelgid.

The history of the Falls of Hills Creek, from the perspectives of geologic processes and Forest Service land management, should encourage everyone to appreciate this scenic gem. It's ours to enjoy due to the works of nature and man.

Happy hiking!

CHAPTER 18

The Wild Beauty of White Oak Falls

For a long time, my wife Phyllis and I have enjoyed the search for "wild beauty." By wild beauty, I don't mean beauty that is reckless, disorderly, or dangerous. I mean the beauty of the wilds, of the untouched beauty that you can stumble upon by simply taking a path less traveled. When we chose byways and bushwhacked paths, I didn't realize at first that we were in pursuit of wild beauty. But when I read this quote by John Muir, "To the sane and free, it will hardly seem necessary to cross the continent in search of wild beauty, however easy the way, for they find it in abundance wherever they chance to be," I knew just what he was talking about. Beauty is where you find it, and it's generally found close at hand in unspoiled and untrammeled lands–in the wilds. Southern West Virginia is, in my opinion, blessed with an abundance of wild beauty largely because much of its unique landscape is protected by an assortment of national, state, and private parks and preserves. Many of these lands are well known such as the New River Gorge or Babcock State Park. But in this chapter, I'd like to feature the wild, almost mystical, beauty of White Oak Falls and a lesser known place called the "Brush Creek Preserve."

Brush Creek Preserve

The Brush Creek Preserve is neither highlighted on maps nor marked by conspicuous signs; nevertheless, it has much to offer. It covers 124 acres in a quiet, yet scenic corner of Mercer County, WV.

The easiest access to the preserve is off Interstate 77. North bound from Princeton, WV, take exit 14 at Athens Road/State Route 20 and turn right at the end of the exit ramp. After 0.1 miles, turn left on Eads Mill Road and continue for 3.3 miles. At this point make a hard right-hand turn onto Brush Creek Falls Road and make about a half a mile descent to a bridge over Brush Creek. Park at the picnic shelter just beyond the bridge. South bound on Interstate 77, take exit 20 at Camp Creek. Turn right onto US 19 then take the next left, which is called Eagle Crest Rd. After less than a quarter mile you'll cross over Interstate 77. After crossing the Turnpike, take the first right-hand turn onto Eads Mill Road. After about three miles on Eads Mill Road, take a road to the left called, "Brush Creek Falls Road." Descend into the canyon; cross the creek; and park at a picnic shelter just beyond the bridge (GPS: Lat. 37.46478, Long. -81.06404).

From the parking area and picnic shelter, which are state-owned, follow an old, rocky road downstream about 0.3 miles to Brush Creek Falls. That's right, on the way to the Brush Creek Preserve and White Oak Falls, there's yet another visual feast–Brush Creek Falls. My jaw dropped the first time I saw this waterfall. I couldn't believe such a lovely, large, and accessible waterfall had escaped my attention for so long. The falls span the width of Brush Creek and are about 33 feet high. A few smaller drops precede the main fall. The Brush Creek watershed is substantial and supports good flow in summer. While it begins as a shallow, meandering stream, Brush Creek swells to river size and cuts a 400-foot deep canyon by the time it reaches the falls. Twenty-four acres surrounding Brush Creek Falls are now managed by the State of West Virginia as part of Pipestem Resort State Park.

Beyond Brush Creek Falls, the rough and rocky road becomes a very comfortable trail with a gentle slope and easy tread. The Brush Creek Preserve begins about a tenth of a mile beyond the falls. In keeping with its low-profile, you could enter the preserve without knowing it. A small sign tacked to a tree on one side of the trail and a blue blaze on the other side mark the preserve boundary. Several yards beyond, four posts straddle the trail to hinder four-wheelers.

The remainder of the trail through the preserve parallels Brush Creek following it all the way to its confluence with the Bluestone River.

Simple Pleasures

There are many simple pleasures to enjoy in this out-of-the-way preserve. One is "water music," that is, the mountain melody of water rolling over rocks. The music serenades you the length of Brush Creek. Another simple pleasure is wild flowers. My wife and I are amateurs at wild flower identification; nevertheless, we saw eastern bottlebrush grass, agrimony, deptford pink, rattlesnake plantain, St. John's wort, naked-flowered tick trefoil, plus a number of flowers that we haven't yet identified. Besides common wild flowers, according to its web site the preserve is home to some uncommon plant species as well including "white cedar, Canada yew, shale barren onion (a regional endemic), and the globally rare shrub Canby's mountain-lover." Being a geologist, I enjoy the sandstone cliffs that line the mountain side of the trail. The cliffs are intricately dissected by fractures and in places gloriously painted by red, brown, yellow, and dark gray iron-bearing minerals. After following Brush Creek for about a mile, the trail makes an abrupt right turn to meet and follow the Bluestone River. The Brush Creek Preserve ends shortly after making this turn.

The Nature Conservancy

But the story of the Brush Creek Preserve doesn't end here. Indeed, you might be surprised to learn that this preserve, this little slice of the wilds tucked away in Mercer County, is part of a nonprofit, global organization called The Nature Conservancy. The mission of The Nature Conservancy is "to preserve the plants, animals and natural communities that represent the diversity of life on Earth by protecting the lands and waters they need to survive." Founded in 1951, the Conservancy works in all 50 of the United States and more than 30 countries. In West Virginia alone The Nature Conservancy oversees a dozen nature preserves including the Brush Creek, Bear Rocks, Cranesville Swamp, Greenland Gap, Hungry Beech, Ice Mountain,

Murphy, Panther Knob, Pike Knob, Slaty Mountain, Upper Shavers Fork, and the Yankauer Preserves. The work of The Nature Conservancy is supported by the donations of more than one million members. It's gratifying to me that wild beauty in a multitude of forms is being protected in all corners of West Virginia by private citizens from various regions and walks of life.

White Oak Falls

Although White Oak Falls does not lie within the Brush Creek Preserve, it's surely worthy of protection. As mentioned above, the lands of the Brush Creek Preserve end as the trail turns at the confluence of Brush Creek and the Bluestone River. This turn is about a mile from the parking area, and if you're willing to walk another mile on the trail, you'll be rewarded with a look at White Oak Falls. The extra mile, so to speak, is not difficult. Being an old railroad bed, the grade is gentle and very even. And since it parallels the Bluestone River, more water music serenades you as you hike. The trail ends at the shores of the Bluestone where White Oak Creek meets the river. The lower falls of White Oak Creek begin right at the Bluestone, where White Oak Creek makes a couple of short drops and runs before flowing into the river. The upper falls, barely visible from the bottom, are sheltered by a large rock amphitheater protected on both sides by steep slopes. Looking up at the falls, the right-hand side seems to be the easier path to the amphitheater. But there is a tight spot where you must hug a small round cliff to get upstream. It's easier, but riskier. The left-hand side requires more climbing, mostly on steep soil slopes, but I believe with a good pair of hiking boots, it's the safer way.

Either way, getting a closer look at the falls is worth the effort. The falls begin with a single drop that fans out into a multi-tiered cascade. The volume of water isn't necessarily impressive, but the form is. And so is the height. From the top ledge to the base pool, I estimate a drop of 50 feet. In addition, as White Oak Creek exits the amphitheater to descend to the Bluestone River, it flows over a number of small falls and short cascades. One of the rock ledges met on the downward fall has been carved into many cylindrical potholes. One of these potholes has an opening at the bottom that splits the falls into two parts–half the water shoots inward and the other half outward. You have to see it to know what I mean, but it's not something seen often at waterfalls. It's yet another facet of the beauty of the wilds.

No wonder we call West Virginia "Wild and Wonderful." Wild beauty abounds here. Brush Creek Falls, The Brush Creek Preserve, and White Oak Falls are just some of those beauties. I hope you find the time to enjoy them.

Happy Trails!

CHAPTER 19

The Wild and Wonderful Meadow River

Towering sandstone cliffs, a boulder-lined riverbed, and rolling whitewater rapids–sounds like the New River. But it isn't. And there's more. A rock walled grotto, a 30-foot sandstone pinnacle, a little stone chapel, a couple of waterfalls, and if the season is right–an ice angel. Where is this place? I'm referring to the Lower Meadow River. In some respects, it's like the New River and then some. Indeed, if I had only one day to hike in Southern West Virginia, I'd head for the Meadow River. It offers so much and is so accessible. If you've never been there, then let me point out a couple of hikes and points of interest along the Meadow River.

A Wild Mountain River

The headwaters of the Meadow River lie in northern Summers County, WV. The river is fed by a series of glades, meadows, and wetlands known as the Big Meadows, from which the river gets its name. Although born in the serenity of meadows and glades, the Meadow River's last few miles are anything but calm. Indeed, the lower reaches of the Meadow River capture so much of what is wild and wonderful about West Virginia. As the Meadow River approaches its confluence with the Gauley River at Carnifex Ferry, it picks up slope and speed. The last six miles of the river drop at a rate of 94 feet per mile. By comparison, the Upper Gauley River drops 28 feet per mile, and on the best stretch of whitewater on the New River the slope is about 20 feet per mile. By any standard, the Meadow River's last run is swift and steep.

So how do you get to this wild river? It's surprisingly easy. The best access is at the Kevin Ritchie Memorial Bridge, which crosses the Meadow River on U.S. Highway 19. (The West Virginia Legislature named the bridge in honor of Kevin Ritchie, a 34-year-old EMS paramedic who was killed in the line of duty while assisting accident victims on the bridge). While driving U.S. 19, I noticed from time to time a few cars parked off the berm just north of the bridge (GPS: Lat. 38.15305, Long. - 80.92434). I made a mental note to check it out some day. And my only regret is that I didn't do it sooner. As it turns out, this is a great spot from which to explore the Meadow River both upstream and downstream. By the way, if you enjoy exploring areas that are off the beaten path, then be watchful for parking spots such as this one. They may lead you to some interesting places.

Rather than park off the highway, though, I recommend turning west on Underwood Road, which is the first intersection north of the bridge. Then take Dietz Road, which is an immediate left turn, and park at the pull out at the curve at the top of the hill. Hike down the dirt road that parallels U.S. 19. After passing a waterfall on your left, a few yards further down look for an obvious fork in the road. It's next to a large rock outcrop with an overhanging ledge. The left fork is the best way to explore the Meadow River upstream, which I'll cover later in this chapter. Take the right fork to explore the rock cliffs and Meadow River downstream.

A Surprise Around Every Turn

My wife Phyllis and I have spent many a happy hour hiking the cliffs of the New River Gorge; yet, we both prefer the cliffs bordering the Meadow River. They are unsurpassed in beauty, size and variety. To me, they're a constant source of delight and discovery. Around every turn of the cliff, it seems, lies a surprise. It might be a bold rock buttress, a sheer cliff face, a waterfall, a cave, or an overhanging rock ledge that defies gravity. Sometimes the features are small, such as intricately carved weathering patterns etched into the sandstone cliffs or mosaics of red and brown hues created by the weathering of iron-bearing minerals in the rocks. The cliffs are rich with beauty and variety.

The downstream cliffs are called "The Main Meadow" in Steve Cater's latest guidebook of rock climbing routes in Southern West Virginia (*New River Gorge, Meadow River and Summersville Lake: Rock Climber's Guidebook, Third Edition*). An excellent resource for hikers looking for new and interesting places, Cater's book is available online at Amazon or at Tamarack in Beckley, WV. To find the Main Meadow, continue down the right-hand fork of the dirt road. As you proceed, the cliffs of the Main Meadow will be on your right and close to the road. But don't charge into the brush right away to reach the cliff face. Wait until you come to a wide spot in the dirt road where ATV's have made ruts around a mud hole. Then look to the right for a slightly worn path leading straight to the cliffs.

Exploring the Main Meadow Cliffs

If you have followed directions, you'll be at the base of the first set of cliffs called the "Tan Wall" where the climbing routes begin. From here the challenge is to follow the base of the cliff line for about a half a mile to the "Moon Wall," which is at the end of the Main Meadow section. Though not a long trail, it is challenging nonetheless because it isn't marked. Rather the way has been made by rock climbers exploring the cliffs. Some sections of the trail are level and flat along linear stretches of the cliff line. But occasionally the cliff line breaks down, and boulder fields and rhododendron hinder progress. When picking your way through these difficult stretches, a good rule of thumb is to hug the cliffs. And along part of this path, I mean that quite literally.

I won't describe the details of this portion of the hike because I'd rather that you savor the discoveries for yourself. I must mention, though, that there are two waterfalls along the way. They only have water during the spring or after heavy rainfall in the summer. But they are good landmarks. The end of the Main Meadow cliffs is about 900 feet beyond the second waterfall. After reaching the end, double back until you find one of several paths that lead back down to the dirt road. There's a short, easy path about 150 feet east of the second waterfall.

A Gateway to the Lower Meadow River

Once on the dirt road, you can double back to the parking area or press on to the banks of the Meadow River, which are just a little way down the road. At the Meadow River, the dirt road intersects what looks like an old narrow gauge railroad bed. The main line railroad formerly ran on the south side of the river, but is now being converted into a rail trail. But this little relic of bygone logging days running on the north side provides a gateway to the Meadow River. It runs downstream beyond the road intersection for about a mile. Along the way, you'll encounter two areas where the railroad bed has slipped away into the river. Don't let these breaks in the road deter you. Continue until you reach a true dead end. Phyllis and I tried to bushwhack beyond the end, but all we got for our efforts were a lot of scratches and a case of poison ivy.

Along this downstream stretch, the Meadow River is as rough and rugged as any West Virginia mountain stream. The grade steepens; the gorge narrows; the whitewater builds; and the boulders just get bigger. Some of the boulders are as big as a house. Brave men and women have kayaked this portion of the Meadow, but only at great risk. This section of the river has claimed the lives of three expert paddlers and may be the most dangerous stretch of whitewater in West Virginia. Though dangerous to kayak, the Meadow River is a thrill to watch. During high water, the rolling waves and thunderous rapids are exhilarating. And even in low water, its boulder lined bed and tree lined banks are beautiful.

But there's more to the Meadow River. Upstream another set of striking sandstone cliffs are definitely worth exploring because they hide a surprise or two. To access the river upstream, take that left-hand fork in the dirt road that I mentioned earlier in the chapter. The road descends to the Meadow River and ends below the U.S. 19 bridge. It intersects the narrow gauge railroad bed, which continues upstream. To explore the upstream cliffs called the "Upper Meadow Walls," hike the railroad bed for about three quarters of a mile. Look for a faint path breaking off to the left toward the cliffs. If you come to a little camp by the river's edge, you've gone too far. Backtrack about 80 paces to find the trail to the cliffs.

Surprises Along the Upper Meadow Cliffs

The trail leads to the base of one of the tallest set of cliffs that I've seen in the New River Region. Called the First Buttress, it's a vertical to slightly overhanging wall of sandstone some 120 to 140 feet high. The wall is orange and brown from weathering and will have you craning your neck to appreciate it. Continue to the right along the base of the cliffs to the Second Buttress, and remember there are surprises around every corner. In this case, you'll be amazed by a column of sandstone some 30 to 40 feet high. My jaw dropped the first time I saw it. Pinnacles or pillars of stone are fairly rare around here and are exciting to find. This one is mushroom shaped with a tree growing on top. The pinnacle guards the entrance to a deep V-shaped notch in the cliff wall. This secluded cove of stone, called the "Grotto" by rock climbers, has a couple of small caves, some overhanging roofs of stone, and a trickle of water down the back wall. The Grotto is a great place to spend some time.

After leaving the Grotto, continue hiking east along the base of the Second Buttress. Watch the cliff wall carefully, for there's a unique structure carved in the sandstone. Look for a four-foot wide hemispherical shaped hollow in the cliff at about eye-level. The hollow was probably once filled with some softer material such as shale or mudstone. The soft material has eroded away and left a fascinating feature behind. The normally linear bedding layers of the sandstone cliff have been squeezed, sliced, diced, and rolled into an elaborate mosaic of color and stone. It defies description, but I liken it to stained glass windows of a chapel. Because of the rounded roof and stained glass effect, I call this place the "Little Chapel of Stone." To me, this stone structure is a work of art. I could study and reflect upon its subtleties and beauty as much as any lover of the fine arts could relish a painting of a master. The Third Buttress lies through an enclosed passage formed by a large slab of sandstone that has slipped off the cliff and wedged itself against the wall. Wonders abound along the Upper Meadow Walls.

The Fourth Buttress

The fourth and last buttress is a little further upstream. But it's worth the trip. To see it, retrace your steps back to the road that runs along the Meadow River. Take the road upstream for about three-quarters of a mile and watch for the first creek that crosses the road. Follow the creek up to the cliffs of the Fourth Buttress. This buttress is split by a small stream that cascades over the cliff and makes a lovely little waterfall. It was in this small cove cut by the stream that I saw the ice angel that I mentioned at the beginning of this chapter. The ice angel, or ice apparition to some, was the remains of a large icicle that had grown on the cliff wall. Warm temperatures and sunshine had carved this mass of ice into an elegant sculpture hauntingly human in form. From the Fourth Buttress, the return trip to the parking area is about two miles.

But if you're like me, you'll be back on the Meadow as soon as you can. The wonders abound; the beauty is abundant, and the river is wild and wonderful.

Happy Trails!

CHAPTER 20

New River Drys: Reflections of the Past

On a glorious summer day in June, my wife, Phyllis, and I decided to celebrate our wedding anniversary with a hike. We picked the trail to the base of Hawks Nest Dam, which was new to us, and set out in search of adventure. We weren't disappointed. After walking for a mile, we emerged from a forest trail into an exotic landscape, quite unlike anywhere else in West Virginia. Giant boulders the size of pick-up trucks, leaning awkwardly upon one another, were strewn across a flat sandstone pavement. The sandstone bedrock, though mostly flat, was in places intricately scoured and sculpted into shallow bowls, deep furrows, or rounded ridges. Even the mighty New River looked odd. Instead of surging powerfully between its banks, it meandered lazily among quiet, emerald-green pools. And scattered along the riverbed were hundreds of isolated, shallow pools lined with tiny wildflowers. This was a landscape to behold. The New River had been tamed. But what had we stumbled upon? As we discovered later, Phyllis and I had been introduced to a wondrous stretch of the New River called "The Drys." We've returned to The Drys many times since that first encounter. In this chapter, I'll share some of the things I've learned about The Drys that make it unique and point out some ways to enjoy it.

The Pages of Our Past

"America is a great story, and there is a river on every page" (Charles Kuralt). In West Virginia, it's the New River that has written the pages of our past. Like many great American rivers, the New River has worn away our mountains, carved our canyons, and leveled our plains. It has molded our landscape and our way of life. The New River is a natural thoroughfare along which roads and rails, cities and towns, mines and factories have been built. It's also an ancient river whose waters ran while the ancestral Appalachian Mountains were uplifted. During its formation, the New River sliced powerfully down through the bedrock of the ancient Appalachian Mountains as they rose. By keeping pace with the uplifting mountains, the New River preserved its ancient, sinuous course, and is now the only river in the Eastern United States that flows northward from the Appalachian Mountains and into the Ohio River drainage. How did the New River accomplish the feat of carving across mountains? And where can the remnants of that mighty engine of erosion best be seen? The best place that I am aware of is The Drys where the carving power of the New River is laid open and bare.

The Hawks Nest Dam Trail

Indeed, The Drys are called that because along this stretch the New River is, well, dry, a mere trickle. The Drys are created by Hawks Nest Dam, which straddles the New River just below Hawks Nest State Park. Here the awesome flow of the New River is not only held in check by the dam, it's also diverted. The Hawks Nest Dam and reservoir, completed in 1934, were designed to generate electric power by diverting the waters of the New River underground for three and a half miles through a rock-carved tunnel varying from 32 to 44 feet in diameter. Tragically, at least 476 men died, primarily to contracting acute silicosis while excavating the tunnel–making it the deadliest industrial accident in the State of West Virginia. At the downstream end of the tunnel, the water emerges at a power plant on the banks of the New River where it drives four large turbines. The tunnel at Hawks

Nest is capable of diverting water at a rate of 10,000 cubic feet per second. Most of the time, this diversion rate exceeds the flow of the New River. So as a rule about 90% of the flow of the New River is diverted into the underground tunnel, and the remaining 10% is allowed to trickle down the river bed forming the fascinating New River Drys.

The Drys are accessed a couple of ways. For your first taste of The Drys, I suggest taking the Hawks Nest Dam trail as Phyllis and I did. From Hawks Nest State Park, drive three miles west on U.S. Route 60 to the junction of WV Route 16 at Chimney Corner. Turn left onto Route 16 and go another three miles to the bridge crossing the New River at Cotton Hill. Just before you cross the bridge, turn into the trailhead parking area on the left (GPS: Lat. 38.11466, Long -81.14245). Or from Fayetteville, take Route 16 west six miles to the bridge at Cotton Hill. The trailhead is just across the bridge on the right. The trail is owned and maintained by Brookfield Renewable Power. Before you venture on the trail, for safety sake heed the warning signs posted by Brookfield which read:

> DANGER: Dam Upstream. Water may rise rapidly and cover this area at any time without warning. Siren will warn of definite water rise.

Though this sounds ominous, I hope it doesn't deter you from enjoying The Drys. Just stay alert, listen for the siren, and don't stray too far from easily accessed higher ground. On one occasion, Phyllis and I had just spread out a picnic lunch on a rock by the river when the siren sounded. Even clutching cans of soda and unwrapped sandwiches, we moved easily to higher ground before the water began to rise. Even so, it only rose a couple of feet.

The Hawks Nest Dam trail runs through the forest along a Brookfield Renewable Power service road. At about 0.7 miles, the trail splits from the road and winds downhill and along the river for another 0.3 miles and eventually deposits you at a broad clearing about 500 feet from the foot of the dam. In front of you lies a broad, flat surface of weathered sandstone with giant boulders strewn this way and that. This is the scene that I described at the beginning of the chapter. It will impress you, if not awe you. If nothing else, it begs for exploration, so I suggest that you scramble between the boulders and investigate this museum of stone statues. The stones are so big that rock climbers practice the art of "bouldering" here. We saw one young couple pack in some large foam mattresses and place them at the foot of the boulders. Then, without ropes or pitons, they climbed the stones using only hand and foot holds.

Recreation Abounds

If you're not a rock climber, there's still plenty to do among The Drys. Fishing is popular. The Drys are great for smallmouth bass, rock bass, flathead catfish, and carp. Nature's fishermen like The Drys, too. I've seen duck, Canada Geese, and even a Blue Heron casually wading or paddling in the water for fish. The river bed is also dotted with shallower, disconnected pools of water that have been carved into the sandstone bedrock. These pools are perfect reflecting ponds that both divide and multiply the blue sky, green water, and gray rock like kaleidoscopes. American water willows—a small, delicate, purple and white wildflower—love the quiet water and ring the pools.

During periods of high water on the New River, the Hawks Nest Dam must release the excess flow into The Drys. This transforms the tranquil Drys into a raging river that proves irresistible to kayakers. Here's a quote from a blog by kayaker Adam Johnson: "There is something about the Dries of the New River. I cannot explain it. Whenever the Dries run, the decision of whether or not to go becomes almost automatic."

A Wildflower Hot Spot

If The Drys interest you, I suggest exploring them further. The bed of the New River can also be accessed by two steep offshoots of the Hawks Nest Dam trail at distances of 0.1 and 0.5 miles from the trailhead, and a more gently graded road at 0.6 miles from the trailhead.

Phyllis and I enjoy making a loop by taking the side trail at 0.6 miles down to The Drys and then walking back downstream to the side trail at 0.1 miles. On hot summer days, we like to put on shorts and old tennis shoes and wade in the river. Nothing beats the heat like wandering from pool to pool checking out the wildflowers, watching for ducks or geese, or just feeling the cool water run over our ankles. What's more we found that a sandy beach at the base of the 0.5 miles side trail is a wildflower hot spot. At various times during the summer at the beach or along the shore we've spotted: American water willow, blue wild indigo, bouncing bet, butterfly milkweed, buttonbush, beach morning glory, fringed loosestrife, lizard tail, obedient plant, pasture rose, purple-flowering raspberry, spotted joe-pye weed, spiderwort, spring beauty, St. John's wort, trumpet creeper, water hemlock, whorled rosinweed, and wild petunia. Since Phyllis and I are only amateurs at wildflower identification, I'm sure this list is incomplete.

There's also good access to The Drys on the other side of State Route 16. Pullouts on the west shoulder of SR 16 immediately downstream from the Cotton Hill Bridge provide parking for the Cotton Hill Wildlife Management Area (GPS: Lat. 38.11716, Long. -81.14382), a portion of The Drys overseen by the State of West Virginia. Trails lead from the pullouts down to the river bed where you have at least another mile of The Drys to explore.

Reflections of the Past

As you can see, The Drys have much to offer outdoor lovers of all kinds—from kayakers to climbers, from fishermen to hikers. But I confess that for me, a geologist, the real attraction of The Drys is the story it tells. In the world of Geology, rocks can talk, and rivers can live and die. Indeed, investigating this dry river bed is like walking in a geologic laboratory or a museum of natural history. For example, you can see the raw, erosive power of the New River, which has cut long chutes, worn deep holes, and scoured wide channels in the tough, underlying sandstone bed. You can run your hand over the smooth bedrock surfaces and imagine the abrasive work of sands and stones that, being driven relentlessly by the currents, have rounded and honed the river bottom. The river intimately knows the bedrock over which it flows. It exploits each tiny weakness in the underlying strata and carves a little deeper into it leaving a slight groove or impression. The result is an irregular, undulating surface of exquisite form. And if a few rocks collect in a shallow depression, the flow of the river can whirl the stones around and around and grind out a pothole. The waters tirelessly work on the river bed and bit-by-bit wear it down. So while standing among The Drys you can catch a glimpse of the awesome and ancient force of the New River that has tamed mountains, carved gorges, and flowed against the grain of the Appalachian Mountains for millions of years.

But there's another river at The Drys. It's not the New River at all. It's an ancient river or rather a system of rivers that passed through this land some 300 million years ago. They drained an ancestral Appalachian Mountain range and eventually wore them into plains. Though the rivers are long since gone, they left remnants of those ancient mountains behind in the vast cliff-forming sandstones of the New River Gorge. Geologists have named the layered formations forming the high cliffs at Hawks Nest the Upper and Lower Nuttall Sandstones. The massive sandstone layers forming the river bed at The Drys is called the Pineville Sandstone. While walking The Drys you can see evidence of the rivers that laid down the sediments of the Pineville Sandstone. The most noticeable features are cross-beds, which as their name suggests, lie at angles to the relatively horizontal layers of sandstone. The cross beds formed by sloping sand bars that shifted either downstream or laterally along the river course. Rounded quartz pebbles imbedded in the sandstone indicate that originally angular rocks were worn smooth by many miles of tumbling and rolling along the river bed. With the mind's eye, these features resurrect those ancient rivers.

As you stroll down The Drys, you walk among many rivers, old and new, and can glimpse reflections of the past in the present. I believe that's what I enjoy most about it. I'm reminded of the closing words of Norman Maclean's novel, *A River Runs Through It*:

> Eventually, all things merge into one, and a river runs through it. The river was cut by the world's great flood and runs over rocks from the basement of time. On some of the rocks are timeless raindrops . . .

The New River Drys is a place to ponder as well as to play. That's what I like about it.

CHAPTER 21

Sandstone Falls: A World Class Waterfall

One fine summer day I found myself face-to-face with what has been called one of the Seven Wonders of West Virginia. I stood in front of and no more than a stone's throw from a mass of rushing mountain water as grand as anything I'd seen before. Volumes of water that dams are built to hold back, rushed directly toward me, leapt over a stony ledge only to turn aside at the last second, and flow harmlessly beneath my feet. At the same time I felt both utterly safe yet completely in awe of the power flowing before me. I was standing at the brink of Sandstone Falls. I'd like to share this place with you and urge you to explore it for yourself. The endeavor is neither difficult nor risky. But you must have a taste for adventure and a willingness to wander off the beaten path.

Sandstone Falls is not difficult to find. It's part of the New River Gorge National River and is listed on just about every visitor's guide and road map of Southern West Virginia. In fact, I found it listed on a worldwide database of waterfalls on an Internet site. And I found out why it was globally recognized. By volume of water, Sandstone Falls is ranked 30th in the world! And by width it's 17th.

A World Class Waterfall

This world class waterfall is right in our own backyard. To get there take the River Road (State Route 26), which begins at the west end of the Route 20 bridge in Hinton. Take it slow on the River Road because it's mostly one lane, and there are residences and camps along the road. Besides, there are plenty of good viewpoints of the New River along the way, including a roadside picnic area at Brooks Falls, about half way up the road to Sandstone Falls. About 8.5 miles up the River Road, you'll come to the National Park Service's Sandstone Falls facility (GPS: Lat. 37.75935, Long. -80.90498). Besides picnickers, hikers, and sightseers, this day use area attracts fishermen, too, looking to catch smallmouth bass and catfish.

But the real attraction is the falls, and the Park Service has made them easy to view. A wooden boardwalk, which minimizes erosion and makes the area accessible to all visitors, winds for about 500 feet between the rocks and trees below the falls. Observation decks along the boardwalk provide several views of the falls. The boardwalk ends at the last observation deck, which showcases a lovely if somewhat distant view of the main falls. For the majority of visitors, a tour of Sandstone Falls finishes here, at the end of the boardwalk, and that by itself would be rewarding. But if you're willing to venture off the boardwalk and do some exploring of your own, there's a way to experience these falls as few people do.

The Best Vantage Point for Viewing the Falls

The key to seeing Sandstone Falls up close and at its best lies in the unique arrangement of the falls. Indeed, it's the way the river is laid out at the falls that lends itself to views that would otherwise be impossible. Due to a hard stratum of rock, called the Stony Gap Sandstone by geologists, the New River narrows at the falls to less than half its full width. In fact, it's a 10 to 25-foot ledge of the Stony Gap Sandstone that creates Sandstone Falls. Because this sandstone is so resistant to the erosive power of the river, the New River has been forced to the southeast side of its bank to make room for several large, flat islands of Stony Gap Sandstone that extend into the river from the northwest bank. Without these islands, you would have to be content to stand on the bank of the river and squint to see the main falls because they would be more than three football fields in length beyond you. But by using these islands like giant stepping stones, it's possible to reach vantage points in the very middle of the New River. In effect, the islands allow you to stand on dry land in the middle of the New River and view Sandstone Falls head on and only a few feet in front of you. A world class waterfall at your feet—you can't beat that!

So how do you get to such a vantage point? Just a few feet before the end of the boardwalk at the main falls observation deck, there's a path leading to the right (west). It leads to a shallow water crossing and onto the next island west. At this point, I prefer to bear a little to the left and head toward the river bank. This takes you to two more small water courses that separate the islands and puts you on the lead island that sits right in front of Sandstone Falls. By the way, the ease of these water crossings depends upon the volume of water flowing in the New River. When the river flow is 3,000 to 5,000 cubic feet per minute, the creeks can be crossed by simply rock hopping. But at higher flows such as 7,000 to 10,000 cubic feet per minute, you're going to have to plan to do some wading. The currents aren't strong in these little creeks, and I haven't felt unsafe crossing them. On the other hand, wading or playing in the New River or around the falls can be very dangerous, and drownings do occur there. The best way to find the flow of the New River before visiting it is at a website maintained by the U.S. Geological Survey. Try this web address for the New River flow at Thurmond, WV: http://waterdata.usgs.gov/wv/nwis/uv?site_no=03185400.

A Fountain of Life

By the way Sandstone Falls is rarely, if ever, overcrowded. Two years ago, my wife Phyllis and I picnicked there on the 4th of July. That day the sky was sunny, and the temperature was just right. The parking lot held a few more cars than usual, but there was plenty of room for all the picnickers, hikers, and fishermen. In fact, when Phyllis and I reached the island in front of the falls, we pretty much had them to ourselves. That's what I like about the state parks and public lands of West Virginia; there are truly places where you can "get away from it all." On the other hand, visiting parks in neighboring states has sometimes been disappointing. I have felt at times as if I traded a crowd in the city for a crowd in the country. But this is not so in West Virginia. John Muir once wrote: "Thousands of tired, nerve-shaken, over-civilized people are beginning to find out that going to the mountains is going home; that wildness is a necessity; and that mountain parks and reservations are useful not only as fountains of timber and irrigating rivers, but as fountains of life." To me the state parks and public lands of West Virginia are indeed, "fountains of life," and Sandstone Falls is at the headwaters.

Once on the leading island, I head for the falls first. They can be viewed along the full length of the upstream edge of the island, which is fortunate, because Sandstone Falls is not just one waterfall, but many. The main falls are more than 800 feet wide and are composed of many segments each having a unique character. To me Sandstone Falls is like a multi-faceted jewel; all its many faces dazzle and delight the eyes. The falls beg for a camera and will keep any photographer entertained for hours trying to capture the essence of its power and beauty.

More Than Just a Waterfall

But there's more to Sandstone Falls than the falls. For instance, if you carefully observe the bedrock, you'll be able to see the mighty hand of the New River at work. The rugged sandstones of the islands have been scoured into shallow, rounded bowls, carved into chutes, and sculpted into a variety of rounded forms. Barry Bryson, a preacher friend of mine, discovered a perfectly cylindrical hole about a foot in diameter cut straight through a six-foot slab of sandstone. Driftwood that has been stranded at the falls makes an interesting study, too. Massive logs beaten by weather, water, and rock lie strewn about the surface and are reminders of the power of the New River. Some of these logs are front rows seats in which to watch the water rush on by. These logs are great "make-shift" picnic tables, too. Nothing beats munching on a sandwich in the middle of the New River with Sandstone Falls right in front of you.

Sandstone Falls has a lot to offer those interested in plant life. According to the National Park Service Brochures, the ecosystem at Sandstone Falls is a "rare Appalachian Flatrock plant community which includes sedges, cedars and pines. This plant assemblage occurs on flat sandstone ledges along the New River and is dependent on the scouring caused by occasional flooding for its long-term integrity." A quarter-mile trail developed by the Park Service will help you explore this unique ecosystem. The trailhead is on the left just beyond the observation deck of the lower falls. The animal life around the falls is also fascinating. Pools of water lying in the shallow bowls and chutes carved in the bedrock teem with life. And on one of our visits, my wife Phyllis and I spotted a blue heron fishing below the falls. Moreover, he was sharing the fishing grounds with a Canada goose. The sight of these two feathery fishermen is one I won't soon forget!

In just about every way, Sandstone Falls is unique. It's a world class waterfall. And it's right in Southern West Virginia just waiting for you to explore.

Happy trails!

GPS Coordinates for Key Locations

Place	Chapter	Lat	Long
Babcock: Skyline Trailhead	1	37.98336	-80.94322
Cathedral Falls	2	38.15389	-81.17967
Hawks Nest Trailhead, Ansted	2	38.13070	-81.10131
New River Drys: Hawks Nest Dam Trailhead	2	38.11466	-81.14245
Pipestem State Park: County Line Trailhead	3	37.52466	-80.98839
Kumbrabow State Forest	4	38.63292	-80.02257
Camp Creek State Park	4	37.50368	-81.12774
Beartown State Park	4	38.05152	-80.27526
Watoga State Park: North Entrance	5	38.11388	-80.09316
Watoga State Park: West Entrance	5	38.12679	-80.17384
Fern Creek Falls Trailhead	6	38.06756	-81.07188
Kaymour Miners Trailhead	6	38.04601	-81.06837
Kaymour Trailhead	6	38.05950	-81.08051
Diamond Point Trailhead #1	7	38.06298	-81.05682
Diamond Point Trailhead #2	7	38.05982	-81.04953
Beauty Mountain Parking	8	38.06022	-81.03593
Beauty Mountain Trailhead #1	8	38.05862	-81.03509
Beauty Mountain Trailhead #2	8	38.04592	-81.02440
Long Point Overlook	9	38.21040	-80.87435
Long Point Trailhead	9	38.23387	-80.86593
Pirate's Cove Trailhead	10	38.24603	-80.85629
Whippoorwill Road	11	38.23220	-80.85063
Douglas Falls	12	39.12403	-79.51965
Kennedy Falls (approx.)	12	39.12033	-79.52036
Blackwater Canyon Overlook	12	39.11464	-79.52442
Canaan Valley	13	39.04506	-79.44585
Beall Trailhead: Canaan Valley	13	39.06361	-79.41805
Middle Valley Trailhead: Canaan Valley	13	39.09667	-79.36317
Valley Overlook Trailhead: Canaan Valley	13	39.13560	-79.33287
Bear Rocks: Dolly Sods	14	39.06611	-79.30154
Beaver Dam Trailhead	14	39.05304	-79.30947
Germany Valley Overlook Cabins	15	38.70722	-79.41194
Gauley River: Laurel Creek Falls	16	38.21430	-81.02950
Gauley River: Ramsey Branch Falls	16	38.20100	-81.01260
Falls of Hills Creek Trailhead	17	38.17809	-80.33861
Brush Creek Falls Trailhead	18	37.46478	-81.06404
Meadow River Trailhead	19	38.15305	-80.92434
New River Drys: Hawks Nest Dam Trailhead	20	38.11466	-81.14245
Cotton Hill Wildlife Management Area	20	38.11716	-81.14382
Sandstone Falls Parking	21	37.75935	-80.90498

CPSIA information can be obtained
at www.ICGtesting.com
Printed in the USA
BVHW09s2238150718
521693BV00010B/124/P